AF522606

CURRICULUM DEVELOPMENT ON DISABILITY STUDIES

CURRICULUM DEVELOPMENT ON DISABILITY STUDIES

By

Gajendra Narayan Karna, PhD (JNU)

DISCOVERY PUBLISHING HOUSE PVT. LTD.
INDIA

Published by:
Namit Wasan
DISCOVERY PUBLISHING HOUSE PVT. LTD.
4383/4B, Ansari Road, Darya Ganj
New Delhi-110 002 (India)
Phone : +91-11-23279245; 23253475; 43596065
E-mail : discoverybooksindia@gmail.com
discoverypublishinghouse@gmail.com
namitwasan9@gmail.com
web : www.discoverypublishinggroup.com

***First Edition:* 2019**

ISBN: 978-93-86841-85-8

Curriculum Development on Disability Studies

Published under the joint auspices of Society for Disability and Rehabilitation Studies (New Delhi, India) & Human Rights and Disability Studies Programmes, School of International Studies, Jawaharlal Nehru University, New Delhi, India

Printed at:
Infinity Imaging Systems
Delhi

Preface

When I joined the M. Phil./Ph.D. programme of study in International Organisaton in January 1988 at the School of International Studies of the Jawaharlal Nehru University (New Delhi) and opted for research in the emerging area of disability and human rights falling under the rubric of Disability Studies under the guidance of Late Professor K.P. Saksena, there was little awareness in Indian universities and academic institutions about the emerging field of Disability Studies as a distinct academic discipline; which had started taking deep roots in the Western academia. Scholars and professionals, transcending disciplinary boundaries, had begun to evince keen and passionate interest in the analyses of laws, regulations and the programmes/schemes affecting the persons with disabilities from inter-disciplinary paradigm. The phenomenon of disability was no longer perceived in terms of personal state of affairs, as the traditional approach (individual-centred) does in confining the study strictly to the individuals so affected, and thereby undermining it as something which concerns the physical and cultural environment within which disabled individuals live.

Thanks to the growing social and political movements of disabled people world-wide during the decade of 1970s, there has been a radical shift in social perception. As a result, disability is now largely viewed as an outcome of the interactions between individuals and environment, rather than as a personal deficit or deficiency. The evolution of Disability Studies as a separate field of academic discipline reflects the change in the conceptual framework of disability. During recent years the increasing pace of globalisation and liberalisation have also tremendously influenced the academia.

Thus, the emerging field of Disability Studies, based on the experiences of the disabled persons, has contributed immensely to understanding disability as also evolving a pedogogy. The development of Disability Studies as an interdisciplinary field of academic inquiry could be visualized as the academic and philosophical aspect of disability rights movement. While disability rights movement constitutes the body, the academic discipline of Disability Studies represents the soul or essence of the movement for empowering the persons with disabilities.

Insofar as the Indian scenario is concerned, though Disability Studies was granted recognition as an academic discipline by the Ministry of Human Resource Development, Government of India long back in September 2005 and the UGC was directed to extend support to universities and colleges in setting up special Department/Centre on Disability Studies as also instituting Rajiv Gandhi Chair in Disability Studies in Central Universities. It was also further reinforced by the 11th Five-Year Plan Working Group on Disability. Notwithstanding all these developments, the UGC has not taken as yet even the basic initiative of constituting a Model Curriculum Development Committee on Disability Studies (as has been done in the case of Gandhian Studies, Human Rights, Dalit Studies and other academic disciplines). Meanwhile, more than seventeen universities/academic institutions (including TISS, IGNOU, JNU and DU) have moved towards launching Disability Studies programmes, though in a haphazard manner because of lack of model curriculum.

Against this background, this book is intended to examine critically the progress made in regard to promotion of teaching and research on Disability Studies, and thereby making a modest, but sincere attempt, to develop a model curriculum on Disability Studies for various programmes of studies being offered by Indian Universities and Academic Institutions. The first ever publication of its kind, this book seeks to make a modest contribution to the existing literature on Disability Studies. As I hope, this book will cater to the long-felt requirements of those faculty, researchers, students and rehabilitation professionals from cross disciplines (including Rehabilitation Science, Community and Social Medicine, Special/Inclusive Education, Political Science, Sociology and Human Rights) who are interested in taking up career in Disability Studies at undergraduate, post-graduate and doctoral levels in universities and higher education institutions, apart from administrators, policy makers and disability rights activists.

A word about the method. This work is the product of several years of painstaking individual research and contemplation in the old-fashioned sense, rather than the so-called modern sophisticated research mechanism. This study is largely based on analytical approach, and has been undertaken with the help of downloaded materials related to curricula on Disability Studies through internet for various programmes of studies (ranging from post-graduation and MPhil to PhD and PG Diploma with focus on Rehabilitation Technology programmes) being offered by universities/ academic institutions around the globe and other relevant literature-such as, books, memoirs, research articles and newspaper clippings.

In course of completion of this write-up, I have been assisted by innumerable people and it is not possible for me to articulate my indebtedness to them all. However, my foremost thanks and indebtedness are due to Late Dr A.P.J. Abdul Kalam (former President of India) who played a key role in getting Disability Studies recognized as a full-fledged academic subject by the Ministry of Human Resource Development/Government of India in September 2005 at the initiative of the Society for Disability and Rehabilitation Studies (New Delhi) under my leadership.

I also take the opportunity to express my sincerest gratitude to Professor M. Jagadesh Kumar (VC, JNU, New Delhi), Professor Sudhir Kumar Sopory (noted scientist at ICGEB & formerly VC, JNU, New Delhi) and Professor

Yogesh Kumar Tyagi (VC, University of Delhi) for always motivating me to delve deep into the area of Disability Studies. My heartfelt indebtness is also due to certain noted medical experts-including Dr Somashekhar S.P. (Oncological Surgeon) and Dr Amit Rauthan—Medical Oncology (both from Manipal Comprehensive Cancer Centre, Manipal Hospital, Bangalore) as also Dr N.R. Dash (Department of Gastrointestinal Surgery, AIIMS, New Delhi) and Dr Asheem Dhall (Director & Head, Cardiology, ISIC, New Delhi) for giving me a fresh lease of life after severe and prolonged indisposition caused by peritoneal cancer followed by cardiac arrest during medication (still continuing). I would be failing in my moral obligation if I don't acknowledge the valuable contribution of Late Professor Bimal Prasad (India's ex-Ambassador to Nepal and a retired Professor of SIS, JNU) in my strugglesome academic sojourn.

I also owe a debt of gratitude to a galaxy of scholars including Professor Rajesh Rajagopalan (Professor of International Politics & Director, Human Rights and Disability Studies Programmes, School of International Studies, JNU, New Delhi), Professor M.S. Varma (Department of Political Science, LNMU, Darbhanga), Professor G. Lokanadha Reddy (Dean, School of Education & HRD, Dravidian University, Kuppam, Andhra Pradesh), Professor P.R. Ramanujam (STRIDE & formerly Pro-VC, IGNOU) and Dr. S.K. Prasad (Dy. Chief Commissioner for Persons with Disabilities/Govt. of India); who deserve thanks from my innermost for stimulating me to develop curriculum in the field of Disability Studies.

I also wish to express my sincere thanks to my colleagues, friends, well-wishers and volunteers at the SDRS (including Raman, Ajay, Ranjan, Sanjay, Pankaj, Shyam and Raj Kumar) who helped me technically in all possible ways. The Director of Discovery Publishing House Pvt. Ltd. Shri Tilak Wasan deserves special thanks and appreciation for launching a Disability Studies Series and carrying out the publication of this work at a very short notice.

Lastly but not less importantly, I cannot but acknowledge the constant co-operation and encouragement of my wife Sandhya, sons-Anurag, Abhigyan and daughter Astha; who have endured all hardships and vicissitudes while I have been constantly undergoing prolonged treatment for peritoneal cancer.

Gajendra Narayan Karna, PhD (JNU)

Human Rights and Disability Studies Programmes,
School of International Studies,
Jawaharlal Nehru University,
New Delhi, India

Contents

1

Introduction

Disability is a perennial global phenomenon transcending class, nation and wealth (Goodley, 2011, p. 1). Around 650 million population in the world is affected by physical, mental or sensory impairments (Disabled World, 2018: World Report on Disability, 2011). Out of this more than 400 millions live in rural and inaccessible parts of developing societies like India, amidst appalling poverty, isolation and frustration (Government of Kerala, p. 3). In the aftermath of disability rights movement, disability issue has catapulted to the centrestage as an issue of 'civil rights'. Consequently, the tone and tenor of global disability discourse has witnessed dramatic change and the issue of disability has metamorphosed from a purely individual centered medical/clinical problem to a socio-political and human rights or rights- based issue. The process of globalization and liberalization has also given a new impetus to the disability rights movement (Karna, 2001, pp. 17-20).

The development of Disability Studies as an inter-disciplinary field of academic inquiry could be visualized as the academic and philosophical aspect of disability rights movement. Both of them are closely intertwined with each other. While disability rights movement constitutes the body, the academic discipline of Disability Studies represents the soul or essence of the movement for empowering the persons with disabilities (Government of Kerala, 2010, p. 3).

The study and analysis of the phenomenon of disability as difference is not new. The disabled have been oppressed, marginalized and stigmatized in almost all societies throughout centuries. They constitute a section of the population, which is most backward, least served and grossly neglected. To put it simply, the persons with disabilities represent the poorest of the poor and the weakest of the weak, who have been socially, educationally and economically disadvantaged, thus having been customarily denied their right to self-assertion, identity and development.

There is, still, a relatively low level of theorization on disability and rehabilitation issues from human rights paradigm in Indian perspective. Adequate and since effort has not been made to concentrate on analysis of social and cultural contexts of disability. Like Women's Studies, Muslim/Islamic Studies, Tribal Studies and Dalit Studies, this field considers disability as a social minority group with an emphasis on the way in which disability is normally constructed culturally, politically, and economically, rather than the traditional emphasis on the physiology of impairment (Government of Kerala, 2010, pp. 3-4). Following the social constructivist view, the proponents of Disability studies maintain that the persons with disabilities are first and foremost individuals (not body parts, not problems to be solved, not objects, and not pathetic) bestowed with the same rights and responsibilities as everyone else. This model supports the viewpoints, ideas, and experiences of all enlightened citizens as also those who get up everyday and deal with their disability in this culture as the experts in what that means.

Despite these limitations, the phenomenon of disability should not be viewed merely as a global medical/clinical problem, but also as a developmental and human rights or rights- based issue. Public policy has, over the years, moved from providing institutional arrangement for education (including technical and vocational) for the children with disabilities and rehabilitation programmes to empowering the persons with disabilities. Especially since the decade of 1970s, the growing social and political movements of disabled persons worldwide have tremendously influenced disability and rehabilitation policies. As the disability rights movement has consolidated, so the language of the mainstream establishment has also undergone changes (Karna: 2001, pp. 17-21). New legislations have been enacted by almost all the countries in order to mainstream the persons with disabilities in national and international developmental activities. In parallel with developments in disability sector, there has been several path-breaking changes in policy orientation with increasing focus on rights-based perspective, poverty reduction and the Millennium Development Goals.

However, the extent to which changes in legislation and documentation have culminated in empowering the disabled individuals in reality is quite debatable. There cannot be denying the fact that defining disability is not an easy task because it is not a fixed category. Rather it is a fluid situation that depends not only on the context in which it is defined, but also who defines it (Withers, 2012, p. 3). Many definitions have been advanced, founded on diverse values and theoretical underpinnings. These definitions could be, roughly, divided into two main categories: (a) the individual centred paradigm and (b) the socio-political paradigm. The difference between both these paradigms lies in substance as also in the subject matter. While according to the former paradigm, problems faced by the disabled individuals are directly related to their disabling conditions. Contrary to this, the socio-political paradigm regards the physical and social environments as major determinants of disability. In other words, the individual paradigm normally locates the problem within the individual and is obsessed with the pursuit of perfect body and mind. On the other hand, the socio-political paradigm locates the problem in society (Karna, 2001, pp. 37-56).

The individual - centred and socio-political paradigms could be further divided into various sub-categories — such as, medical/clinical, psychological, economic vocational, systems analysis, minority group, socio-political and human rights. Thus, disability has been, traditionally, examined from medical/clinical approach that focuses on functional impairments; or from psychological approach with its orientation on psychological disturbances; or from economic-vocational standpoint that stresses vocational limitations arising out of physical, mental or sensory impairments; or from systems analysis approach which views the phenomenon of disability in systemic terms; or from minority group perspective which seeks to justify analogy between the disabled and other minorities; or from socio-political approach which regards disability as a product of interactions between individual and environment. Lastly, the human rights or rights-based approach to disability perceives legal measures as constituting the fundamental framework by which equalization of opportunities could be ensured to such disadvantaged individuals. (Karna, 2001, pp. 37-56)

It is interesting to note that there is considerable amount of similarity between the socio-political and human rights approaches. While the socio-political approach visualizes disability as having stemmed primarily from the failure of a structured social environment (to adapt to the needs and aspirations of the disabled individuals) rather than from the inability of disabled individuals to come up to the expectations of the society deeply obsessed with the notion of normality and bodily perfection. On the other hand, the human rights approach to disability views the persons with disabilities as subjects of law and as an issue of equalization of opportunities. The basic goal is to empower the persons with disabilities and ensure their active participation in political, economic, social, and cultural life in a way that is respectful and accommodating of their differences. In other words, the disability rights debate is not so much about the enjoyment of specific rights. Rather, it is about ensuring the equal effective enjoyment of all human rights, without discrimination to the persons with disabilities. (Government of Kerala, 2010, p. 5)

However, certain scholars and experts of Disability Studies have also criticized this approach on the ground of negativeness. Given that protective legislation is based upon a formal rather than redistributive model of social justice, it has been criticized for attempting to tackle the barriers that deny the disabled individuals access to equal opportunities, without addressing the structural disadvantage from which those barriers are created. Negative attitudes, limited physical access, restricted access to communication and/or resources and to the rights and privileges of a social group — are the major barriers which interfere with the disabled individuals to actualize his/her desired roles. Thus, disability is, basically, determined by 'public policy'. Disability is whatever policy wants and makes it to be. This observation corroborates the fact that disability is a problem or a disadvantageous situation, necessitating compensatory or ameliorative action. (Government of Kerala, 2010, p. 6)

The complexity of defining disability has, however, aggravated because of indiscriminate and loose use, by scholars, of terms like 'impaired', 'disabled', 'physically handicapped'/'physically challenged', 'mentally challenged' and 'differently abled'. Though the fact remains that there is classical distinction in the meaning of these terminologies, they all convey some or other disabling situations and provide a fragmented perspective of disability. The most accepted terminology from rights-based perspective is 'persons with disabilities' (United Nations, 2006; Government of India, 2016) or 'disabled persons'. Following this framework, Disability Studies could be defined as a field of knowledge or academic inquiry, which reformulates the study of disability by perceiving it as a social phenomenon, social construct, metaphor and culture, and thereby suggesting adoption of rights-based perspective (Karna, 2001, p. 250). Disability Studies is primarily centred on how disability is defined, viewed and represented in society.

Ironically, despite plethora of studies and research carried out in developed societies, the area of disability studies, still, remains quite grey and unexplored. It continues to be ignored in the curricula of schools, colleges and universities in India and due attention has not been given to address issues related to disability and rehabilitation policies from inter-disciplinary paradigms. This could be reflected in the way the plethora of degrees and diploma courses are restructured over the years by national institutes with sectoral perspectives with medical/clinical orientation. (Government of Kerala, 2010, p. 6)

This tendency has resulted in the issue of disability being studied and analysed as merely the part of the syllabi of certain specific disciplines such as, medical science, bio-technology, psychology, social work, special education, community health, rehabilitation medicine, labour economics and sociology and that, too, in a piecemeal fashion. Moreover, there is far too rigid a compartmentalisation of disciplines in the curricula of Indian Universities and academic institutions, which has contributed to a reduction of cross-flow between various fields of research and obstructed progress in the specific field of disability. Since disability is basically a human rights and developmental issue, its multitudinous dimensions must be approached from interdisciplinary paradigm (Karna, 2001, p. 19; Government of Kerala, 2010, p. 7).

Against this background, the idea of bringing out a book on "Curriculum Development on Disability Studies" has been mooted with a view to provide ground work for scholars, experts, rehabilitation professionals, educational administrators and policy planners for systematically launching programmes of studies on Disability Studies at various levels ranging from post-MA/MSc and MPhil to PhD and PG Diploma levels. Ideally, the Centre(s)/Department(s) on Disability Studies should undertake academic, research, training and extension activities in order to actualise the goal of empowering the persons with disabilities at the grassroots level. (Government of Kerala, 2010, p. 7)

Among the major activities and roles identified for such Centre(s)/Department(s) could be imparting teaching and research at the level of MA/MSc, MPhil and PhD programmes in Disability Studies with interdisciplinary perspectives; offering One and half year PG Diploma in Disability Studies (with Concentration on Innovations in Rehabilitation Technology); organising short-term and long-term vocational training as also orientation/refresher programmes for the faculty, scholars and stakeholders as also rehabilitation professionals/technocrats respectively; developing resource materials for the use by persons with disabilities as also professionals and social activists for delivery of services to the stakeholders; conducting institutional and community rehabilitation programmes; establishing better linkages between university and government/non-governmental organisations working in disability sector; acting as a cleaning house on various disability aspects in terms of assistance, promotion of research and dissemination of information; conducting innovative research for promoting inclusive education practices at school and college level for students with disabilities; carrying out participatory action research on issues of contemporary relevance in disability sector; espousing for incorporation of disability, rehabilitation and human rights related issues/contents into the curricula of subjects being taught at school and college levels; and most importantly sensitizing at the grassroots level about the imperativeness of changing the mindsets of society. (Government of Kerala, 2010, pp. 7-8)

Since the courses to be offered by the centres/ departments should be multidisciplinary in nature, development of interdisciplinary team of experts/ professionals would be necessary. Imparting courses on Disability Studies as part of higher education involves expertise from plethora of academic disciplines.

This way a modest effort could be made for striking a proper balance between the contemporary theory of Disability Studies and Rehabilitation Technology as also their applicability in empowering the persons with disabilities. Apart from academic programmes, the faculty, staff and students involved with these centres should also actively engage in research, training and development of psycho-educational tools. Briefly stated, the basic policy goals underlying these academic programmes are to address the four major guiding principles of the interdisciplinary field of Disability Studies. (Government of Kerala, 2010, pp. 8-9)

Philosophy: Disability Studies is grounded in rights-based or empowerment model of disability, or a social constructivist view. The theoretical underpinning for offering Disability Studies courses is to deconstruct what is assumed, to make way for new ideas, new voices, and new views/ perspectives.

Voice: Disability Studies uses a personal voice, a subjective voice to tell stories and explain and explore the lived experiences of those affected by some or other disabling situations. That personal voice is inclusive and by virtue of its mass appeal, demonstrates the value, capability and power of persons with disabilities. That personal voice means that what the persons with disabilities feel or experience about disability as stakeholders constitutes an integral part of this branch of knowledge. This should, however, not be misconstrued to mean that the persons without disabilities do not or should not have any role to play with regard to theory- building and development of this discipline.

Interdisciplinary: In order to understand 'disability' in true perspective, it is highly imperative to examine it from a variety of perspectives. What can sociology, psychology, history, political science and economics tell us about disability? What do linguists and anthropologists perceive about disability? How do policy makers, analysts, and lawyers visualize disability? What can educators, rehabilitation professionals/specialists, and social workers teach us? How do nurses, doctors, and therapists support an understanding of disability? Typically, only one of these views has been considered at a time, in a specific course of study. This merging of views creates a broader and more complete understanding of disability.

Independent: Lastly and most importantly, it must be borne in mind that Disability Studies has become an established field of interdisciplinary academic inquiry and a rallying point for disability rights activists globally. One may find plethora of reference and textbooks for Disability Studies courses. These texts are relatively new, published mostly since the decade of 1970s and substantially authored by scholars from Western countries. There are also abundance of literature-such as, books, chapters and articles written by the stakeholders—i. e. the persons with disabilities about their own experiences. There are books that chronicle the growth of disability rights movement. Furthermore, there are large number of professional bodies/organizations focused on developing the core field of Disability Studies from interdisciplinary perspectives.

Insofar as attracting the best students for the programmes are concerned, a national level entrance test (on the pattern of JNU, IIM and other premier academic institutions) should be held in major cities of the country to select the competent candidates with interest in pursuing the career in Disability Studies. Another important way to encourage talented and promising students/scholars for opting academic, research and professional career in Disability Studies could be to institute certain scholarships/fellowships. There could be adequate scope for degree holders in Disability Studies for employment avenues in central and state universities, colleges, national institutes, organisations and donor agencies working in disability sector at national and international levels. Those who achieve excellence in research at doctoral level could also stand good chance of getting the Fulbright and Commonwealth Fellowships for advanced career in Disability Studies in foreign universities/academic institutions. For exceptional scholars with outstanding contribution to Disability Studies, there could also be scope for applying for the most prestigious Ed Roberts Post-Doctoral Fellowship for higher research in the USA.

Thus, the most important step required to be taken by UGC and MHRD/Government of India is to achieve the basic goal of promoting teaching, research, training and extension programmes in the area of Disability Studies in universities and academic institutions of the country.

Given the gargantuan dimension and complex nature of the problem of disability in India, the greatest need of the hour is neither more programming nor even specific entitlements for the persons with disabilities, but a re-orientation of policy framework of disability from rights-based approach. Despite launching of plethora of schemes/plans and investing crores of rupees by Government of India on physical and vocational rehabilitation as also legal empowerment, the goal of mainstreaming the persons with disabilities into society and nation- building is still as far way as ever. There is a wide gap in policy formulation and implementation (Government of Kerala, 2010, p. 11).

Though there is lack of accurate and reliable data on disability in India, it could roughly be assumed that not less than ten per cent of the total population are affected by physical, mental and sensory impairments and around 75 per cent of the total population is concentrated in rural, hilly and far-flung backward regions of developing countries. The drive for national survey on disability is underway for the forthcoming Census 2021 and the outcome is being awaited keenly by one and all, especially the advocates of disability rights movement.

If the yardstick adopted by WHO/World Bank is taken into account so as to ascertain the quantum of population incapacitated by various disabling situations in our country, it could come around the staggering figure of more than thirteen crore (WHO/World Bank, 2011). Despite so much brouhaha in policy circles over empowerment of the persons with disabilities, the situation is quite alarming at the grassroots level and only a miniscule part of the disabled population has so far been covered by governmental schemes/programmes. Even the scheme benefits do not go to them without pinches because of rampant corruption and red tapism involved in delivery of services. The monitoring and watchdog mechanism put in place has so far failed to ensure delivery of services and justice to the genuine disabled beneficiaries in villages and remote areas.

Thus, Disability Studies is theoretically based on the premise that the disadvantages and barriers typically experienced by the persons with disabilities reflect primarily the way society responds to diverse types of 'differences'. The social knowledge is normally experiential. In the context of movements for social change, this implies that the experience of oppression by the persons with disabilities has culminated in a shared understanding and linkage with other disadvantaged groups. This philosophy synchronizes very well with the oft- repeated slogan of disability rights movement— "nothing about us without us".

Since disability is basically a developmental and rights-based issue, its multi-faceted aspects must be approached from a holistic interdisciplinary paradigm in keeping with the basic tenet of disability rights movement. Viewed from this perspective, the initiative taken by the Government of Kerala could prove to a milestone; as it has come at a time when there is complete haphazardness with regard to imparting teaching and research in the field of Disability Studies even in those universities (such as, IGNOU, TISS, Punjab and other universities) where programmes of studies have been started or are in the process of getting started (such as, JNU, DU, Mizoram, Gauhati and other Universities). The development of curriculum on Disability Studies for various programmes of studies (ranging from MA/MSc and MPhil to PG Diploma with focus on Rehabilitation Technology) effort could greatly stimulate the faculty, scholars, rehabilitation professionals and disability rights activists to take up career in Disability Studies for further accelerating the pace of empowerment of the persons with disabilities.

2

Development of Disability Studies as an Academic Discipline

The disability rights movement has significant impact on both academia and policy makers. The inter- disciplinary (and counter-disciplinary) field of Disability Studies has emerged from the womb of disability rights movement (Karna, 2001, p. 240). The study of 'Disability Studies' has developed as a separate and interdisciplinary academic discipline in universities, colleges and academic institutions of Western countries — such as, the USA, the UK, Canada, Australia, New Zealand, Sweden, Denmark, Africa, the Middle East and other countries of the world, including certain countries in the Asian continent (such as, India, Japan and Sri Lanka). The degrees and diplomas ranging from certificate/ foundation, graduation and post-graduation to doctorate and post-doctorate are offered in this area. Researchers from diverse professions are evincing keen interest in the analyses of laws, regulations, policies and programmes affecting persons with disabilities and examining the phenomenon of disability from inter-disciplinary perspectives.

Thus, Disability Studies has blossomed into a field of academic investigation so as to address the issue of an "organized critique on the constricted, inadequate and inaccurate conceptualizations of disability that have dominated academic inquiry. But more than that, the critique poses a challenge to the notion that disability is primarily a medical-clinical problem. The moot-point is how to mould the society so as to facilitate the independent living of the persons with disabilities. In other words, Disability Studies seeks to apply social, cultural, historical, political and philosophical perspectives to study the phenomenon of disability in society. The underlying assumption is to approach disability, rehabilitation and human rights issues from holistic and integrative perspective (Government of Kerala, 2010, p. 13). Without an appreciation of policy issues shaping the alternatives available to such disadvantaged people, individuals opting career in health sciences, the helping professions and other occupations are debarred from valuable insights and crucial contexts for their efforts to serve the interests and needs of this under-privileged segment of the population. (Karna, 2001, p. 18)

During the course of the last three and half decades, the disability rights movement has traversed a long way and achieved major policy goals. The most importantly, it triggered off the emergence of Disability Studies during the 1970s and 1980s by organizing advocacy groups and academics. (Government of Kerala, 2010, p. 14). Partly as an attempt to seize this opportunity, the Open University in the UK introduced in 1970 a new course on "The Handicapped Person in the Community" as part of its undergraduate programme. This course achieved enormous popularity and subsequently, it was followed with launching of the first MA program in Disability Studies by the University of Kent. However, a major impetus in this regard was the convening in 1977 of the White House Conference on Handicapped Individuals in the USA. Interestingly, around 3000 persons congregated in Washington, DC in May 1977 to engage in the debate and set up a nation - wide network of advocates. A crucial role in this direction was played by scholars, who were greatly concerned about disability and rehabilitation issues.

One may hardly find such a rare coincidence that one of the beginning articles, authored self-consciously from the perspective of Disability Studies had appeared immediately after the White House Conference. The same year also witnessed the launching of the first course on Disability Studies in the USA. It was in the area of Clinical Sociology primarily focused on the experience of living with disability, a critical life experience generally avoided by many persons. It is also significant to note the background; as the instructor was a disabled individual who helped the students in gaining a better appreciation of policy issues concerning disability and rehabilitation policies and thereby heralding a new era in the development of Disability Studies as a separate academic discipline. The growth of this discipline could be regarded to have formally originated from this vantage point.

The decade of 1990s further expanded the range of Disability Studies with a flurry of courses introduced by a galaxy of universities and academic institutions. According to a rough estimate, more than 125 courses on Disability Studies are currently offered by universities and academic institutions around the globe; while several such programme of studies are on anvil. The degrees and diplomas offered by the universities and academic institutions range from degrees and concentrations to minors and general courses on Disability Studies. One may cite plethora of illustrations in this context. (Government of Kerala, 2010, p. 4).

The Canadian programme in Disability Studies at Ryerson University; an MA degree in Critical Disability Studies at York University; a concentration in Disability Studies for MA or PhD in the Cultural Foundations of Education Programme at Syracuse University; undergraduate and inter-disciplinary minors in Disability Studies in several universities—such as, Ohio State University in Columbus, Ohio, and the University of California, Berkeley; and an interdisciplinary PhD in Disability Studies at the University of Illinois at Chicago. Multidisciplinary Graduate Certificate in Disability Studies is imparted under the aegis of the City University of New York and MA in Deaf Studies, Cultural Studies Concentration and Deaf History Concentration is offered by Gallaudet University.

There are a stream of other prestigious universities and academic institutions conducting courses on Disability Studies, some of which are – Pacific University (Disability Studies in Humanities and Social Sciences – Minor), Columbia University – Teachers College (Master of Arts in Disability Studies in Education - DSE), Washington State University (Undergraduate Minor in Disability Studies), University of Delaware (Undergraduate Interdisciplinary Minor in Disabilities Studies), University of Maine (Undergraduate Disability Studies Core Curriculum and Graduate Interdisciplinary Concentration in Disability Studies), University of Manitoba (Interdisciplinary Master's in Disability Studies), University of Pittsburgh (Graduate Disability Studies Certificate Program), University of Toledo (Undergraduate Interdisciplinary Minor in Disability Studies, Master of Liberal Studies Program—MLS, Concentration in Disability Studies—DST) and University of Washington (Disability Studies Minor).

Moreover, information regarding more than 50 affiliated programmes, centers, clusters and research institutes at different universities has also been recently gathered through web search; which gives the impression that university - affiliated centres are scattered in almost all parts of the globe ranging from the Centre for Developmental Disability Studies at the University of Sydney in New South Wales to the programme in Disability Studies at Rutgers University, where coursework has been restructured so as to incorporate the topic of disability geography. The Centre for Disability Studies at the University of Leeds has been actively working towards promoting teaching and research in the area of Disability Studies. Likewise, the Center on Disability Studies at the University of Hawaii is focused on cultural approaches to disability issues; whereas the Center for Research in Disability and Society in New South Wales offers scholarships to researchers pursuing PhD at Curtin University and Temple University has introduced courses and a graduate certificate program in Disability Studies and Sheffield Hallam University is offering Post Graduate Certificate in Disability Studies.

Based on the information gathered and collated through diverse sources, the detailed list of universities and academic institutions offering degree, diploma and certificate programmes in the field of Disability Studies at different levels is as given below (Karna, 2001; pp. 261-263; Government of Kerala, 2010, pp. 16-18).

List of Disability Studies Courses offered by Universities, Colleges and Academic Institutions*

Brandeis University
California School of Professional Psychology
California State University at Fresno
California State University at Long Beach
Carleton University
Columbia University
Deakin University
Dowling College
Emory University
Flinders University
Gallaudet University
Hobart and William Smith Colleges
Hofstra University
Hunter College
Juniata College
Linköping University
Metropolitan State College
National-Louis University at Illinois
Northern Arizona University
Northern Illinois University
Pacific University
Portland State University
Ryerson University
San Francisco State University
Sheffield Hallam University

Simon Fraser University
Sonoma State University
State University of New York at Plattsburgh
Suffolk University
Syracuse University
The City University of New York
Tufts University
University of Arkansas
University of British Columbia
University of Calgary
University of California at Berkeley
University of Delaware
University of Hawaii at Manoa
University of Illinois
University of Illinois at Chicago
University of Iowa
University of Kansas
University of Maine
University of Manitoba
University of Maryland
University of Massachusetts at Boston
University of Minnesota
University of Missouri at Kansas City
University of Nebraska
University of North Carolina
University of Oklahoma
University of Oregon
University of Pittsburgh
University of Pittsburgh at Johnstown
University of South Carolina
University of Southern Maine
University of Texas at Austin

University of Texas at Dallas
University of Toledo
University of Toronto
University of London
University of Greenwich
University of Leeds
University of Leicester
University of Montana
University of New Hampshire
University of Sussex
University of Wisconsin - Madison
Uppsala University
Utah State University
Washington State University
West Virginia University
York University

Status of Disability Research in India

Ironically, despite plethora of studies and research carried out in developed societies; this area, still, remains quite grey and unexplored; and continues to be ignored in the curricula of schools, colleges and universities in developing societies like India and due attention has not been given to examine disability and rehabilitation policies from inter-disciplinary paradigms. This tendency has resulted in the issue of disability being studied and analysed as merely the part of the syllabi of certain specific disciplines - such as, Medical Science, Bio-technology, Psychology, Engineering, Social Work, Special Education, Community Health, Rehabilitation Medicine, Labour Economics and Sociology and that, too, in a rather piecemeal and parochial fashion (Karna, 2001, p. 241; Government of Kerala, 2010, pp. 13-14).

While significant contribution could also be expected from other disciplines-such as, Anthropology, Political Science, History, Area Studies, Gandhian and Buddhist Studies as also different branches of humanities (including Literature, Philosophy, Religion and Arts). Moreover, there is far too rigid a compartmentalization of disciplines in the curricula of Indian Universities and academic institutions, which has contributed to a reduction of cross-flow between various fields of research and obstructed progress in the specific field of disability (Karna, 2001, p. 241; Government of Kerala, 2010, p. 19).

Disability Studies is an innovative area with sound intellectual and professional foundation in social sciences, humanities and rehabilitation sciences (Karna, 2001, p. 244; Government of Kerala, 2010, p. 19). The theoretical and conceptual armamentaria of these disciplines provide frameworks to understand the persistent themes relating to the critical issues meriting attention, to properly understand the problems of the field and to suggest integrative approaches. The equally significant aspect of Disability Studies education is the social integration or what is commonly referred to as 'empowerment of the disabled individuals'. The mainstream society has always endeavoured to address the issues of inclusion and exclusion, human rights, laws, access to education, the physical and social environment, employment opportunities, disability benefit programmes, science and technology as applied in the case of the persons with disabilities.

An indepth understanding of the ideology, power, and dynamics of these key social actors is required for bringing about change in institutional behaviour. In order to inculcate participatory role among the persons with disabilities, one must have better appreciation of disability and rehabilitation policies. The participatory action research is oriented towards visualizing research as a joint product of discussion between professional researchers and practitioners and consumers. Within the disciplinary area of Disability Studies, it involves members of the target group to be studied in choosing the problem to research, designing the study, and implementing the research field (Government of Kerala, 2010, p. 19).

Scholars and professionals (associated with institutions of higher education) need to evince keen interest in the analysis of laws, regulations and the programs/schemes affecting the persons with disabilities from inter- disciplinary paradigm. Courses and schemes targeted at providing vocational education to the disabled after consultations with experts in the field through a number of regional workshops may be introduced and modified in a broader perspective. Faculties, officials and staffs in universities/institutes may be sensitized to appreciate the problems and barriers encountered by the persons with disabilities. Qualitative vocational and professional training programs may be devised so as to be imparted to all those involved in rendering and delivery of services to the persons with disabilities (Government of Kerala, 2010, p. 20).

The enhancement of professional skills through continuing rehabilitation education programmes could further expand the ambit of Disability Studies. Sensitization by organizing seminars, workshops, conferences as well as mass awareness campaigns through different channels of press and media could immensely facilitate the process of the empowerment of the disabled individuals. Since disability is basically a human rights and developmental issue, its multitudinous dimensions must be approached from interdisciplinary paradigm. The institutions of higher education and intellectuals have to play a onerous role in transformation of societal perception towards disability. Special scholarships/fellowships as also academic exchange/collaboration programmes must be instituted at different levels, especially MA/MSc, MPhil./PhD and Post-doctoral levels, so as to promote further research in this emerging academic discipline. Involvement of scholars and researchers in Disability Studies in institutions of higher education, cutting across disciplinary boundaries, could go a long way in providing a sound theoretical foundation to this emerging field of Disability Studies (Government of Kerala, 2010, p. 20).

The phenomenon of disability among populations is widespread and although plethora of studies on disability has been carried out, there is, however, lack of comparability among countries and even studies conducted in the same country or region. Yet despite a lack of clarity, disability has become a major issue in public policy from the perspective of equal opportunities, the increasing burden of age- related disability, work participation, social security benefits and so forth. One of the main problems is that disability is defined differently for differently so that there is no consistent overview of disability among populations or the implications for disability policies.

Disability policy is faced with two contradictory goals. One is to ensure that disabled citizens are not excluded; that they are encouraged and empowered to participate as fully as possible in economic and social life, and in particular to engage in gainful employment and that they are not ousted from the labour market too easily or too early. The other goal is to ensure that those who are or who become disabled, have income security that they are not denied the means to live decently because of disabilities that may restrict their earning potential. How to reconcile these twin goals is, still, a challenging issue.

On the other hand, the field of Disability Studies is a relatively recent area of academic inquiry with a tendency to cross - disciplinary boundaries. During recent couple of decades, the realization that disability is a cultural phenomenon has gained momentum, along with the disability rights movement as the vehicle for societal change. However, what has not yet been articulated, is the future direction of the disability rights movement. It is interesting to note that the relationship between disability politics and the power brokers in other parts of the world is becoming more clearly established; while the silent majority of the disabled population still remains isolated, uninformed and stigmatized.

From the above elucidation, it is quite clear that Disability Studies has so far become a matured academic discipline with sound theoretical and professional foundation with two major characteristics — firstly, the area of Disability Studies is quite inter-disciplinary in its nature and scope. That is why; the scholars and professionals transcending disciplinary boundaries are passionately involved in this intellectual venture. Secondly, the teaching of this discipline is imparted in the schools and colleges of several Western universities, especially in the USA, UK, Canada, Australia, Sweden, Denmark and a stream of other countries stretching to all parts of the world. Full/Part Time/Visiting/Guest Faculties at the under-graduate and post-graduate levels basically offer the teaching. It may be noted that these concepts are applicable in different circumstances; disability is an experience, which could be traced throughout human societies and cultures. It is not a frail weed growing haphazardly, but also a strong plant, which has come to occupy a prominent position in the field of academia.

The issue of disability and the experiences of disabled people have so far been given scant consideration in academic discourses, particularly in developing societies like India (which has the dubious distinction of being the country with the highest population of the persons with disabilities). There is greater need to infuse into all programmes of studies currently being offered by universities and academic institutions on all typologies of disabilities, their cultures, needs, issues and concerns. Only then could the persons with disabilities be accorded full recognition as equals and be included in housing, transportation, places of public accommodation and recreation, educational programmes and the workforce at par with their able bodied counterparts. However, both the issue and the experiences have been ironically marginalized and only in certain specific disciplines, and that, too, in a rather piece-meal fashion, the area of Disability Studies has been accorded prominent place. Unfortunately, this has proved to be quite counter-productive with the issue of disability being visualized as essentially a medical problem and the experience of disability as being contingent upon a variety of psychological adjustment processes. In order to counter the medical and psychological dominance in this area, ultimately nothing less than a 'social theory of disability' is the pressing need of the contemporary time. The keystone of the disability movement is a collective reappraisal of a devalued identity, a process where problems are depersonalized and translated into political issues.

New Directions for Future

During recent decades, especially in the aftermath of the disability rights movement, disability politics has assumed the form of global 'civil rights movement'. The increasing pace of globalization and liberalization, coupled with wars, industrialization, disease, accidents, ageing and other emerging social problems have contributed to make disability a perennial problem. The burgeoning population of the persons with disabilities has become a continuing global concern. Not to speak of developing societies, even the developed societies have not been able to mainstream the disabled population.

Disability is a denial of citizenship. As long as the problem of appalling poverty, illiteracy and unemployment is not arrested, the goal of empowering the disabled would remain just a myth. In developing societies, where substantial proportion of the disabled population is concentrated, their prospects of securing education and employment are, so to say, the least or non-existent. So much so that even in developed societies, their rate of unemployment is often double than that of their able-bodied counterparts.

Cynics would assume this to be merely a question of lack of opportunity for the disabled and a problem, which requires to be tackled with the overall improvement in the economic sphere. Indeed, such a parochial and discriminatory approach undermines not only their basic human rights but also the economic benefits accruing to themselves, their families and the state itself if they were to be productively engaged into the labour force, thereby mainstreaming them into the fabric of society. It presents a sordid picture in human terms with the persons with disabilities gripped by the feelings of inadequacy, dependency and insecurity, normally relegated to the margin of society for turning to charity or begging as a means of sustenance (Government of Kerala, 2010, pp. 22-24).

The persons with disabilities are truly equal citizens, fully entitled to participate in all areas of political, economic and civic life. They are first and foremost human beings with same basic human needs, privileges and rights as the rest of society. The fulfillment of physiological needs of food, warmth, shelter and sex contribute to self-esteem and personality development. Viewed from this perspective, the problems and barriers faced by the disabled individuals in their practical lives are largely aggravated by the social environment which involves the question of their human rights—the availability of the conditions for the development of the innate characteristic bestowed on him/her by nature as a human being.

The growth of Disability Studies as an academic discipline is one of the most significant contributions of the Twentieth century to the academia. Started as an academic component of disability rights movement during the decade of 1970s, it has become an established academic field of inquiry and brought fresh perspectives for understanding and providing solutions to the problems and barriers faced by the persons with disabilities. The edifice of Disability Studies is based on the assumption that the society must integrate the gargantuan population affected by disabling situations in some or other ways. There is vast and growing literature on the subject which seems to have been largely unperused by decision makers, researchers and social activists. The issue of disability and the experiences of disabled people have so far been given scant consideration in academic discourses (Government of Kerala, 2010, pp. 23-24).

The disability rights movement, which was launched globally by the persons with disabilities and the disability rights activists as a reaction against this apathetic social attitude and parochial considerations, has generated a new wave of identity consciousness among the persons with disabilities. The persons with disabilities as a marginalized group have increasingly applied rights-based arguments to place their issues on the international political radar screen.

As discussed earlier, the teaching of Disability Studies has gained momentum during recent decades as a separate academic discipline in the universities and academic institutions of both the Western and Non-Western countries - such as, the USA, the UK, Canada, Australia, Sweden, Mexico, New Zealand, Japan and Srilanka; and degrees/diplomas ranging from certificate and graduation to doctorate and post doctorate are offered in this area. However, it is quite ironic that despite having the dubious distinction of being the country with the highest population of the persons with disabilities (conservatively estimated to be in the range of more than 100 millions or so), the situation is quite reverse. Notwithstanding, plethora of studies and research carried out on multitudinous aspects of disability and allied issues in developed societies; the field of Disability Studies remains, still, a grey and unexplored area in our country – not having been properly unraveled by intellectuals, social activists as also policy planners and constantly ignored in the curricula of universities and academic institutions.

Insofar as development of Disability Studies in Indian context is concerned, it was granted recognition as an academic discipline by the Ministry of Human Resource Development (MHRD), Government of India in September, 2005 and the clear-cut directive was given to the University Grants Commission for extending support to universities and colleges in setting up special Department/Centre on Disability Studies as also instituting Rajiv Gandhi Chair in Disability Studies in Central Universities. Furthermore, it was reinforced by the 11th Five Year Plan Working Group on Empowering the Disabled (constituted by Planning Commission, Government of India, 2007); which formulated an ambitious scheme for promotion of teaching and research in Disability Studies in academic institutions. The idea got a further boost with the Report of Group of Ministers (constituted by Hon'ble Prime Minister); which came out with two major recommendations: (i) to make all schools, colleges and universities barrier-free and (ii) to promote teaching and research on Disability Studies in Central Universities and Other Academic Institutions.

All these initiatives of the Government of India notwithstanding, the UGC has not taken even the first stage of constituting the Model Curriculum Development Committee on Disability Studies (as has been done in the case of Gandhian Studies, Human Rights, Dalit Studies and other academic disciplines). Meanwhile, certain universities/ academic institutions (such as, IGNOU, TISS, JNU, DU, Periyar, Alagappa, Panjab, Gauhati and Ambedkar) have moved towards launching Disability Studies programmes, though in a haphazard manner because of lack of model curriculum. The reasons for this lackadaisical attitude on the part of intelligentsia are not far to seek; as there is abysmally low level of theorization on disability and rehabilitation issues from rights-based paradigm in Indian perspective. There is, thus, imperativeness of pedagogical development in this unexplored area in our country.

The mounting realisation that disability must be approached from a holistic perspective has yielded a corresponding awareness that knowledge of public policies concerning disabled persons is an essential ingredient for the pursuit of such vocations. The basic idea is to focus attention on promotion of multi-disciplinary academic activities, training programmes and research, apart from documentation and dissemination of research and innovative practices in the emerging field of Disability Studies.

Viewed from this perspective, the initiative taken by the Government of Kerala (with regard to instituting two centres of Excellence on Disability Studies and developing curriculum on Disability Studies for various courses) could prove to a milestone; as it has come at a time when there is complete haphazardness with regard to imparting teaching and research in the field of Disability Studies even in those universities where programmes of studies have been started. This small and modest effort could greatly stimulate the faculties and scholars to take up career in Disability Studies; which could subsequently accelerate the pace of empowering the persons with disabilities (Government of Kerala, 2010, p. 26).

In addition, the University Grants Commission should provide funding to institute Schools/Centre(s)/Department(s) of Disability Studies as also institute Rajiv Gandhi chairs in universities and colleges throughout the country. The Distance Education Council (DEC), IGNOU should also encourage Distance Education Programmes on the core field of Disability Studies and allied areas so as to bridge the vast gap in the required and existing trained manpower. The UGC should be directed to constitute on priority basis a Model Curriculum Development Committee on Disability Studies, consisting of noted experts, scholars, social activists and stakeholders—i.e. the persons with disabilities having grassroots experiences. Other governmental bodies like NCTE, AICTE, NIEPA, DEC, CSIR, and ICAR should also be involved in the promotion of courses/module preparation on Disability Studies in their respective fields and set aside separate budget allocation for this purpose. The Ministry of HRD and UGC should give priority for International Exchange/Collaboration Programmes on Disability Studies and Research. The UGC should also introduce Special Fellowship Scheme for the scholars pursuing higher studies and research in Disability Studies at MPhil, PhD and Post Doctoral levels.

Concluding Observations

Disability Studies is an interdisciplinary field of study, primarily focused on the contributions, experiences, history and culture of the persons with disabilities. The area of Disability Studies, therefore, should be recognized by the Government of India, for all practical purposes, as an academic discipline and be notified for employment opportunities in various sectors, Central/State/Deemed – to - be Universities, National Institutes, Union Public Service Commission, State Public Service Commissions, governmental and non-governmental organizations at both national and state levels. The students/scholars with Graduate, Post Graduate and other Degrees in Disability Studies should be treated at par with the teachers/faculties of other subjects working in schools, colleges and universities and hence, be given equalization of opportunities in employment (Government of Kerala, 2010, p. 27).

Since the disabled constitute ten per cent of the total population in our country. So it is all the more imperative that like Women's Studies, Muslim Studies, Media Studies, Nehru Studies, Gandhian Studies, Area Studies and a vast spectrum of academic disciplines which are the thrust areas of higher education and research, this emerging field of knowledge must attract the attention of policy makers at the Ministry of Human Resource Development and funding agencies like UGC, ICSSR, ICHR, ICPR, ICMR, CSIR, ICAR as also central universities/and academic institutions (Karna, 2001, p. 307; Government of Kerala, 2010, pp. 27-28). There is, thus, an urgent need for various disciplines to focus attention on this neglected field of inquiry from inter-disciplinary orientations. The major problem faced by the sizeable chunk of the population of the persons with disabilities, especially all those living in the rural, inaccessible, hilly and tribal regions of country is the negative social perception with regard to their capability and potentialities. Closely linked with removal of negative social perception regarding disabling situations is eradication of stigma associated with disability.

The intellectuals, policy makers and disability rights activists have onerous role to play in eradicating the misconceptions linked with disabling situations and bringing out social change, thereby facilitating the empowerment of the persons with disabilities. The goal of empowering the huge population of persons with disabilities across the country could not be achieved unless a nation- wide intellectual revolution is launched. Though during the last some years, there has been some conscious attempt in our country to make the planning process more participatory and democratic than the approach adopted earlier, particularly from 1996 to 2004 – the period which saw the intense activities in law making for the disabled (Government of Kerala, 2010, p. 28).

However, as everything else in India, disability rights movement has undergone a period of uncertainty, lack of conceptual clarity, cohesiveness and a firm political will to do something concrete, and the national laws also have been experiencing the same. In this context, adoption of the UN Convention on the Rights of Persons with Disabilities in 2006, followed by its ratification by Government of India in October, 2007 and subsequently enactment of Rights of Persons with Disabilities Act (2016) has the potential to carry forward not only the unfinished agenda but also the urgent imperativeness of reviewing, amending, updating and, if necessary, repealing some of the existing laws or portions thereof.

The promotion of teaching and research in the area of Disability Studies as also incorporation of disability studies contents in curricula at different stages ranging from schools and colleges to universities could greatly facilitate the onward march of disability rights movement in India. Furthermore, the field of Disability Studies provides a unique and divergent vantage point through which scholars, activists and civil society could contribute to generate societal awareness by dispelling age old myths and superstitious ideas related to disabling situations (Government of Kerala, 2010, p. 28). This way Disability Studies could be an effective instrument for changing the mindsets of society and also generating a wave of identity consciousness among the persons with disabilities.

3

Curriculum Development for Suggested Courses on Disability Studies to be offered by Universities/Academic Institutions

Before proceeding further, it seems necessary for us to be familiar with the meaning of 'curriculum'. The term 'curriculum' means many things to many people. 'Curriculum' normally refers to planned learning experiences that the educational institution intends to provide for its learners (Uys and Gwele, 2005, p. 1). Despite the lack of convergence of opinion among the scholars with regard to meaning of the term 'curriculum', there seems to be consensus that educational institutions (as institutions charged with the all important societal function of educating citizens) have the sole claim to curriculum. Furthermore, despite divergence of opinions on other aspects, most agree that in education of all forms, there is no such thing as being neutral (Bode, 1937). Some authors are credited with the view that education should be directed towards helping learners become intelligent and critical citizens in a democratic society (Dewey, 1916, 1961). Stated in simple terms, either the learners have to be taught to fit as a cog into the existing social machinery, or to recognize their own responsibility for the transformation of the social, political and economic world in which they live.

Developing a curriculum is a major task, which should be seen as an ongoing process, rather than a one-off event. No curriculum can develop in a vacuum. It is developed by a group of educators, for a group of students, in a specific academic context. In order to develop a relevant, forward-looking and practical curriculum, the curriculum team needs to make a thorough study of the system in which the curriculum will be embedded. The noted Western educationist Wragg (1997) gives offers three propositions that can be perceived as the rationale for a situation analysis as the first step of the process of curriculum development. To begin with, education must incorporate a vision of the future, since education does not prepare students for today or yesterday, but for tomorrow. A situation analysis therefore has to try to predict what the future holds for those who acquire degree/ diploma in any particular discipline. Accordingly, it has to examine the contemporary trends and movements, and evaluate their strengths and weaknesses. Secondly, there could be growing demands and expectations from people, both in terms of their chosen career as also in the wider global context. What was good enough for us might not be good enough for current students. Thirdly, the learning of students must be guided by several influences, without focusing narrowly on one aspect. The challenge, thus, is how to study the context and the future with a view to basing the new curriculum on evidence and on best-practice.

Significantly, the development of curriculum is not usually done by the Curriculum Committee, but by small teams of teachers or individual teachers entrusted with the responsibility of teaching that specific course. It may be stated that in each course there could be three major impacts on student development: the student, the course and the teacher. The course developers shape the course, and therefore their aims, their beliefs and their competence play a crucial role in shaping the final outcome for the students and the teacher. But more than that, the student also plays a significant role.

Now after having a brief recapitulation about the meaning of the term 'curriculum', let us new go ahead with designing and developing various courses on Disability Studies (ranging from MA/MSc and MPhil to PhD and PG Diploma with focus on Rehabilitation Technology) to be offered by universities and higher education institutions.

MA/MSc in Disability Studies

Master of Arts/Science in Disability Studies (MDS)

The MA/MSc in Disability Studies (MDS) is intended to explore the area of Disability Studies from rights-based perspective. It is quite unique and innovative in that it contributes to emerging participatory action research in Disability Studies by examining critically the systemic social, political, legal and economic barriers to the full and equal participation as also social inclusion of persons with disabilities.

The interdisciplinary approach of the programme is informed by various academic fields – such as, medical science, rehabilitation science, law, anthropology, geography, economics, education, labour studies, political science, social work, sociology, identity politics, women's/gender studies, human rights, refugee and immigration studies, history, arts/aesthetics, architectural engineering, media studies, natural sciences (including environmental sciences), management and gerontology. Theories of human rights form the basis for understanding how existing legal, economic and social policies have failed to eradicate the inequality and oppression faced by the persons with disabilities.

Offered on a full time (two years-four semesters) basis, the MA/MSc in Disability Studies provides an innovative area of study for students with varied background, including persons with disabilities actively engaged in the disability rights movement, civil servants, professionals in the field of disability, and persons working in non-governmental organizations – such as, members of community organizations and advocacy groups.

The objectives of MA/MSc in Disability Studies are as follows:

- To promote interdisciplinary study of Disability Studies;
- To meet the growing demand from students, staff, professionals and organizations for persons with disabilities for an interdisciplinary MA/MSc programme in Disability Studies;

- To offer a comprehensive curriculum covering major scholarly perspectives and professional and ethical issues in disability, human rights, social justice and social policy, and encouraging students to critique existing policies/ programmes and practices;
- To give an insight into rights- based perspective for understanding existing legal, economic and social rationales for inclusion in relation to systemic barriers and oppression faced by the persons with disabilities;
- To provide a structure for career in advanced study and research in the interdisciplinary field of Disability Studies; and
- To enhance and promote employment and capacity building as also skill development avenues for the scholars and professionals desiring to work in disability sector and allied areas.

Eligibility for Admission

Bachelor's degree in any discipline under 10+2+3 pattern of education with at least 55% marks in case of Social Sciences/ Humanities and 60% marks in natural sciences, engineering, medical sciences, management and allied areas.

Degree Requirements

***Minimum credit requirements 72 (Duration: 4 semesters, to be extendable by two extra semesters in special situations; CGPA requirements 4.0)**

The first and second years of the MDS programme (comprising two semesters each of 6 months' duration) would have total 72 credits. The courses are divided into five parts, consisting of ten core papers (10 × 4 credits each = 40 credits), four elective papers (4 × 4 credits each = 16 credits), two practicum (2 × 2 credits each = 4 credits), one internship programme (2 credits) and one dissertation work (10 credits). The break- up of dissertation work is 6 credits for preparation of dissertation, 2 credits for research colloquium/seminar and 2 credits for viva-voce.

For core and elective papers, the credits are to be awarded in the ratio of 80:20, thereby implying that 80 per cent is earmarked for term - end written examinations and 20 for continuous internal assessment by the teachers concerned.

The course titles as also required credits are given (semester-wise):

First Year: Semester-I

- MDS 001: Understanding Disability *(Core paper) 4 credits*
- MDS 002: Introduction to Disability Studies *(Core paper) 4 credits*
- MDS 003: Disability, Human Rights and Social Justice *(Core paper) 4 credits*
- MDS 004: History of Disability *(Core paper) 4 credits*
- MDSP-1 : Practicum 2 *credits*

First Year: Semester-II

- MDS 005: Disability in Indian Culture, Literature and Folklores *(Core paper) 4 credits*
- MDS 006: Psycho- Social Aspects of Disability *(Core paper) 4 credits*
- MDS 007: Disability, Assistive Devices and ICT*(Core paper) 4 credits*
- MDS 008: Disability, Education and Capacity Building *(Core paper) 4 credits*
- MDSP-2: Practicum 2 credits

Second Year: Semester-III

- MDS 009: Disability, Society and Public Policy *(Core paper) 4 credits*
- MDS 010: Research Methodology in Disability Studies *(Core paper) 4 credits*
- MDS 011: Disability, Family Support and Self-Determination *(Elective paper*) 4 credits*
- MDS 012: Disability, Sexuality and Independent Living *(Elective paper) 4 credits*
- MDS 013: Disability and Civil Rights Movement *(Elective paper) 4 credits*

- MDS 014: Disability and Special/Inclusive Education (Elective paper) 4 credits
- MDS 015: Disability and Public Transportation *(Elective paper) 4 credits*
- MDSP 3: Internship programme *2 credits*

Second Year: Semester-IV

- MDS 016: Dissertation Work 10 credits**
- MDS 017: Politics of Inclusion and Exclusion: A Study of Laws and Policies and Programmes *(Elective paper) 4 credits*
- MDS 018: Disability Management and Rehabilitation Technology (Elective paper) 4 credits
- MDS 019: Aging and Disability *(Elective paper) 4 credits*
- MDS 020: Women, Disability and Discrimination *(Elective paper) 4 credits*
- MDS 021: Guidance and Counselling in Disability Studies *(Elective paper) 4 credits*

Notes: *The student has the option to select any two elective papers out of five papers in Semesters-III and IV.

**The break- up of credits for dissertation work – Preparation of dissertation – 6 credits, Research colloquium/seminar – 2 credits, Viva-voce – 2 credits

Semester-I

MDS 001: Understanding Disability

This course provides a broad overview of definitions and paradigms of disability (such as, medical/clinical, psychological, economic-vocational, systems analysis, minority group, socio- political and rights- based); theoretical perspectives–functionalist, role theory, interactionism, disability and human rights issue, and recent developments in feminist and postmodern approaches to disability. Special attention is given to the historical and cultural development of concepts and categories of disability; disability theory and policy at provincial, national and international levels; and implications of theory and practice for the lives of persons with disabilities.

Suggested Readings

Albrecht, G.L. et al (Eds) (2001) *Handbook of Disability Studies* (Thousand Oaks, CA: Sage Publications).

--------(Eds) (2006) *Encyclopedia of Disability* (Thousand Oaks, CA: Sage Publications).

Barnes, C. and Mercer, G. (2003) *Disability* (Oxford: Polity Press).

--------et al (Eds)(1999) *Exploring Disability: A Sociological Introduction* (Cambridge: Polity Press).

Barton, L. and Oliver, M. (Eds) (1997) *Disability Studies: Past, Present and Future* (Leeds: The Disability Press).

Butler, R. and Parr, H. (Eds) (2005) *Mind and Body Space: Geographies of Illness, Impairment and Disability* (London and New York: Routledge).

Dell Orto, A.E. and Marinelli, R. P. (Eds) (1995) *Encyclopedia of Disability and Rehabilitation* (Macmillan Library Reference USA).

French, Sally and Swain, John (2008) Understanding Disability. A Guide for Health Professionals (Philadelphia: Churchill Livingstone Elsevier)

Karna, G.N. (2007) Disability Studies in India: new directions for future, Disability Studies in Higher Education: *Monograph Series No. 2* (New Delhi: Society for Disability and Rehabilitation Studies).

--------(2001) *Disability Studies in India: Retrospects and Prospects* (New Delhi: Gyan Publishing House).

--------(1999a) *United Nations and Rights of Disabled Persons: A Study in Indian Perspective* (New Delhi: APH Publishing House).

--------(1999b) Disabled perspective, *The Pioneer* (New Delhi), Dec. 8.

Kristiansen, K. (2008) *Arguing about Disability: Philosophical Perspectives* (London: Routledge).

Linton, S. (1998) *Claiming Disability: Knowledge and Identity* (New York: New York University Press).

Longmore, P.K. (2003) *Why I Burned My Book and Other Essays on Disability* (Philadelphia: Temple University Press).

Oliver, M. (1996) *Understanding Disability: From Theory to Practice* (Houndmills, Macmillan Pvt. Limited).

--------and N. Watson (2001) *The social model of disability: an outdated ideology?, Research in Social Science and Disability,* 2, pp 9-28.

Perkins, M. (2007) *Pragmatic Impairment* (Cambridge University Press).

Quinn, P. (1998) *Understanding Disability: A Lifespan Approach* (Thousand Oaks: California; Sage Publications).

Roulstone, Alan and Prideaux, Simon (2012) Understanding Disability Policy (Bristol: Policy Press).

Sheila, A. M. M. and Williamson, L. (2007) *Impairment and Disability: Law and Ethics at the Beginning and End of Life* (New York: Routledge-Cavendish).

WHO (1980) *International Classification of Impairments, Disabilities, and Handicaps: A Manual of Classification Relating to the Consequences of Disease* (Geneva).

--------(2001) *International Classification of Functioning, Disability, and Health* (Geneva).

WHO and World Bank (2011) *World Report on Disability* (Geneva), also available at: http://www.who.int/disabilities/world_report/2011/report.pdf (especially chapters 1 & 2)

MDS 002: Introduction to Disability Studies

Disability Studies approaches disability not as an individual tragedy or a medical-clinical problem but as a cultural construct-akin to gender and race-that undergirds social practices and cultural representations in various media. This course draws on various disciplinary perspectives to understand the broad and complex phenomenon of disability in historical perspective, as represented in literature and culture, as also it impinges on issues of broader public concern today.

Suggested Readings

Adams, Rachel et al (Eds) (2015) *Keywords for Disability Studies* (New York and London: New York University Press), especially chapters 1, 2, 52 & 55.

Albrecht, G.L. et al (Eds) (2001) *Handbook of Disability Studies* (Thousand Oaks, CA: Sage Publications).

--------(Eds) (2006) *Encyclopedia of Disability* (Thousand Oaks, CA: Sage Publications).

Barnes, C. and Mercer, G. (Eds) (2002) *Disability Studies Today* (Cambridge: Polity Press).

--------et al (Eds) (1999)*Exploring Disability: A Sociological Introduction* (Cambridge: Polity Press).

Barton, L. and Oliver, M. (Eds)(1997) *Disability Studies: Past, Present and Future* (Leeds: The Disability Press).

Corcoran, Tim et al (Eds) (2015) *Disability Studies: Educating for Inclusion* (Rotterdam: Sense Publishers), especially chapter 14.

Davis, L.J. (Ed.)(1997) *The Disability Studies Reader* (New York: Routledge).

Goodley, Dan (2011) *Disability Studies: An Interdisciplinary Introduction* (Los Angeles: Sage)

Grue, Jan (2015) Disability and Discourse Analysis (Surrey: Ashgate Publishing Limited)

Johnstone, D. (1998) *An Introduction to Disability Studies* (London: David Fulton Publishers).

Karna, G.N. (2007a) Promotion of Disability Studies in Education, *Monograph Series No. 1: Disability Studies in India: Role of Institutions of Higher Education* (New Delhi: Society for Disability and Rehabilitation Studies).

--------(2007b) Disability Studies in India: new directions for future, *Disability Studies in Higher Education: Monograph Series No.* 2 (New Delhi: Society for Disability and Rehabilitation Studies).

--------(2001) Disability Studies in India: Retrospects and Prospects (New Delhi: Gyan Publishing House).

--------(2000) Disability Studies in India: issues and challenges, *International Journal of Disability Studies*, inaugural issue on 'Disability and Social Policy in the New Millennium',1(1), Oct.-Dec., pp. 20-40.

Linton, S. (1998) *Claiming Disability: Knowledge and Identity* (New York: New York University Press).

Longmore, P.K. (2003) *Why I Burned My Book and Other Essays on Disability* (Philadelphia: Temple University Press).

Oliver, M. (1996) *Understanding Disability: From Theory to Practice* (Houndmills: Macmillan Pvt. Limited).

Reddy, G.L. and Poornima, R. (2009) Integration of Disability Studies in general curriculum at school and college levels in India: a critical appraisal, *University News*, 47 (17).

Wappett, Matthew and Arndt, Katrina (Eds)(2013) *Foundations of Disability Studies* (New York: Palgrave Macmillan), especially chapter 1.

Watermeyer, B. et al (Eds) (2006) *Disability and Social Change: A South African Agenda* (Cape Town: HSRC Press).

MDS 003: Disability Human Rights and Social Justice

This paper incorporates the fundamental philosophical, historical and legal concepts surrounding the development and implementation of ideas and policies related to human rights and social justice. It includes a broad understanding of international and national human rights norms and standards as well as cross-cultural interpretations of what is meant by social justice and legal rights obligations. The meaning of human rights and social justice are considered within the context of their applicability to persons with disabilities. Moreover, this paper also examines diversity pertaining to cross-cultural, class, gender, sexual orientation, race, ethnicity, age and poverty issues as they relate to disability. There is a focus on the ways in which diversity issues in the context of broad socio-economic factors impact experiences of persons with disabilities and how equity struggles within a diverse society inter-connect with one another.

Suggested Readings

Baylies, C (2002) Disability and the notion of human development: questions of rights and capabilities, *Disability and Society*, 17(7), pp. 725-739.

Blanck, Peter and Flynn, Ilionóir (Eds) (2017) *Routledge Handbook of Disability Law and Human Rights* (London and New York: Routledge)

Kanter, Arlene S. (2015) *The Development of Disability Rights Under International Law: From Charity to Human Rights* (London and New York: Routledge)

Karna, G. N. (2008) Editorial: Disability rights in a global context, *International Journal of Therapy and Rehabilitation*, 15 (10), 01 October, pp 420-421.

--------(2002) Disability and human rights: An international perspective, *International Journal of Disability Studies*, special issue on 'Disability and Human Rights', 1(1), Jan.-Mar., pp. 3-27.

--------(2002b) Disability and the politics of discrimination, *Human Rights Perspective*, 1 (1), pp.

--------(2001) Disability Studies in India: Retrospects and Prospects (New Delhi: Gyan Publishing House).

--------(2000a) Impaired rehabilitation, *The Pioneer* (New Delhi), Jan. 24.

--------(2000b) Disabled human rights, *The Pioneer* (New Delhi), Feb.11.

--------(1999) United Nations and the Rights of Disabled Persons: A Study in Indian Perspective (New Delhi: APH Publishing Corporation).

--------and Gaharana, K. (1994) Disability and the rights of disabled persons, In: K.P. Saksena (Ed) *Human Rights: Perspective and Challenges beyond 1990s* (New Delhi: Lancer Books).

Krieger, L.H. (2003) *Backlash against the ADA: Reinterpreting Disability Rights* (Ann Arbor, MI: University of Michigan Press).

Lazar, Jonathan and Stein, Michael Ashley (Eds) (2017) *Disability, Human Rights, and Information Technology* (Philadelphia: University of Pennsylvania Press)

McNeese, Tim (2014) *Disability Rights Movement* (Minneapolis: ABDO Publishing Company)

Nussbaum, M.C. (2006) *Frontiers of Justice: Disability, Nationality Species* Membership (Oxford University Press).

O' Brien, R. (Ed) (2004) *Voices from the Edge* (Oxford University Press).

Rispler-Chaim (2007) *Disability in Islamic Law* (The Netherlands: Springer).

Riddle, Christpher A. (2017) *Human Rights, Disability, and Capabilities* (New York: Springer)

Rioux, Marcia H. et al (Eds) (2011) *Critical Perspectives on Human Rights and Disability Law* (Leiden and Boston: Martinus Nijhoff Publishers).

United Nations (2006) *United Nations Convention on Rights of Persons with Disabilities* (New York: United Nations).

--------(2007) From *Exclusion to Equality: Realizing the Rights of Persons with Disabilities*, Handbook for Parliamentarians on the Convention on the Rights of Persons with Disabilities and its Optional Protocol (Geneva).

MDS 004: History of Disability (Compulsory 4 credits)

This course would examine the historical experiences of persons with disabilities from ancient and medieval world as also Indian history to the emergence of disability rights movement since the decade of 1970s. Topics to be covered include: pre-industrial interpretations of physical and mental disability; the impact of the industrial revolution on disability as a social category and lived experience; segregation, trans-institutionalization and community living; rehabilitation programmes and their critics in the twentieth century; diversity, discrimination and activism within the disability community; and the modern development of critical literature on the history of persons with disabilities.

Suggested Readings

Albrecht, G.L. et al (Eds) (2001) *Handbook of Disability Studies* (Thousand Oaks, CA: Sage Publications).

--------(Eds) (2006) *Encyclopedia of Disability* (Thousand Oaks, CA: Sage Publications).

Braddock, D.L. and Parish, S.L. (2001) An Institutional History of Disability, In: Gary L. Albrecht et al (Eds) *Handbook of Disability Studies* (Thousand Oaks, CA: Sage), pp. 11-68.

Bragg, L. (1997) From the mute God to the lesser God: disability in medieval Celtic and Old Norse literature, *Disability & Society,*12, pp.165-177.

Bryan, W.V. (2006) *In Search of Freedom: How persons with disabilities have been disenfranchised from the mainstream of American Society and how the search for freedom continues* (Springfield, Illinois: Charles C. Thomas Publisher Limited).

--------(2007) Multicultural Aspects of Disabilities: A Guide to Understanding and Assisting Minorities in the Rehabilitation Process (Springfield, Illinois: Charles C. Thomas Publisher Ltd.).

Carcopino, J. (1940) *Daily Life in Ancient Rome: The People and Their City at the Height of the Empire* (New Haven, CT: Yale University Press).

Dasen, V. (1995) *Dwarfs in Ancient Egypt and Greece* (Oxford, UK: Clarendon).

Finkelstein, V. (1980) *Attitudes and Disabled People* (New York: World Rehabilitation Fund).

Garland, R. (1995) *The Eye of the Beholder: Deformity & Disability in the Graeco-Roman World* (Ithaca, NY: Cornell University Press).

Goodey, C.F. (1999) Politics, Nature, and Necessity: Were Aristotle's Slaves Feeble Minded?, *Political Theory,* 27(2), pp. 203-223.

Groce, N. (1985) *Everyone here spoke sign language: Hereditary Deafness on Martha's Vineyard* (Cambridge, MA: Harvard University Press).

Haggard, H. (1932) *The Lame, the Halt, and the Blind: The Vital Role of Medicine in the History of Civilization* (New York: Blue Ribbon Books).

Hanes, Roy et al (Eds)(2018) *The Routledge History of Disability* (London and New York: Routledge).

Karna, G.N. (2001) *Disability Studies in India: Retrospects and Prospects* (New Delhi: Gyan Publishing House).

--------(1999) *The United Nations and Rights of Disabled Persons: A Study in Indian Perspective* (New Delhi: APH Pub. Co.).

Longmore, P.K. and Umansky, L. (Eds.) (2001) *The New Disability History: American Perspectives* (New York University Press).

Metzler, Irina (2013) Disability in Medieval Europe: Thinking about Physical Impairment during the high Middle Ages, c. 1100-1400 (London: Routledge).

O'Brien, R. (2001) *Crippled Justice: The History of Modern Disability Policy in the Workplace* (Chicago: University of Chicago Press).

Ogden, D. (1997) *The Crooked Kings of Ancient Greece* (London: Duckworth).

Olyan, S.M. (2008) *Disability in the Hebrew Bible: Interpreting Mental and Physical Differences* (Cambridge University Press).

Rose, M. (2003) *The Staff of Oedipus:Transforming Disability in Ancient Greece* (Ann Arbor: University of Michigan Press).

Safford, P.L. and Safford, E.J. (1996) *A History of Childhood & Disability* (New York: Teachers College Press).

Siraisi, N.G. (1990) *Medieval & Early Renaissance Medicine: An Introduction to Knowledge and Practice* (Chicago: University of Chicago Press).

Skinner, P. (1997) *Health and Medicine in Early Medieval Southern Italy* (Leiden, the Netherlands, and New York: E.J. Brill).

Stiker, H. (1999) *A History of Disability*, translated by W. Sayers (Ann Arbor: University of Michigan Press).

Turner, David M. and Stagg, Kevin (Eds) (2006) Social Histories of Disability and *Deformity: Bodies, Images and Experiences: Routledge Studies in the Social History of Medicine* (Oxon: Routledge)

Wright, David (2011) *Downs: The History of a Disability* (OUP)

Wright, D. and Digby, A. (Eds) (2002) *From Idiocy to Mental Deficiency: Historical Perspectives on People with Learning Disabilities* (London: Routledge), rep.

MDSP-1: Practicum – The theme and modality of the practicum shall be decided by the concerned teacher.

Semester-II

MDS 005: Disability in Indian Literature and Culture

This course is intended to explore the representation of disability related fantasies and fictions in Western as also Indian literature and culture. The overriding concerns of the course will be with how the body's shape and capacities have been assumed to determine character and fate, how physical and mental impairments have been used in literature to signify moral and psychological states, and how representation may challenge conventional conceptions of "normality" and "disability." Through critical discussion of major literary works, discussion would focus on the ways in which our perceptions of the body and our definitions of disability have underpinned our concepts of humanness; our cultural perceptions of what bodies should be or do. Literary texts from various periods will be supplemented with some non-literary texts and documentary films.

Suggested Readings

Akhilnanda, C. (1952) *Mental Health and Hindu Psychology* (London: George Allen).

Alur, M. and Rioux, M. (2000) *Included: An Exploration of Six Early Education Pilot Projects for Children with Disabilities in India* (UNICEF, South Asia Regional Office, India, 2000).

Anthony, M, J. *(1999) Rights of Persons with Disabilities (New Delhi: Indian Social Institute, New Delhi, 1999).*

Awasthi, S.K. (2000) *Rights of Unsound Mind Accused* (Pune: C T J Publication).

Despouy, L. (1993) *Human Rights and Disabled* (New York: United Nations).

Dhanda, A. (2000) *Legal Order and Mental Disorder* (New Delhi: Sage Publications).

Government of India (2005) *Disability Manual* (New Delhi: NHRC).

--------*(2006)* Report of Working Group on Empowering the Disabled for Eleventh Five-Year Plan (New Delhi: Planning Commission).

--------(undated) *Know your Rights: Rights of Persons with Disabilities* (New Delhi: NHRC).

--------(undated) *Discrimination based on Sex, Caste, Religion and Disability* (New Delhi: NHRC).

Iyer, V.R.K. (1982) *Law, Justice and the Disabled* (New Delhi: Deep & Deep).

Johnston, Kirsty (2016) *Disability Theatre and Modern Drama: Recasting Moderrism* (London: Bloomsbury).

Karna, G. N. (1999) *United Nations and the Rights of Disabled Persons: A Study an Indian Perspective* (New Delhi: A.P.H. Publishing Corporation).

--------(2008) Disability rights in a global context, editorial, *International Journal of Therapy and Rehabilitation*, 15(10), Oct., pp 420-421.

--------(2002a) Disability and human rights: an international perspective, *International Journal of Disability Studies*,special issue on 'Disability and Human Rights', 1(1), Jan.-Mar., pp. 3-27.

--------(2002b) Disability and the politics of discrimination, *Human Rights Perspective*, 1 (1).

Kumari, Sandhya (2018a) 'A Sociological Study of Disabled Characters as Depicted in Hindi Prose' (in Hindi), PhD

Thesis submitted to Jawaharlal Nehru University, New Delhi, India (unpublished).

--------(Ed)(2018b) Collection of Disabled Character-based Hindi Stories-in Hindi (unpublished).

Mitchell, D. and Snuder, S. (2001) Representation and its Discontents: The Uneasy Home of Disability in Literature and Film, In: Gary L. Albrecht et al (Eds) *Handbook of Disability Studies (Thousand Oaks,CA: Sage).*

Nussbaum, M.C. (2007) *Frontiers of Justice* (New Delhi: Oxford University Press).

Pandey, S. and Chirimar, Priyanka (2005) *Disability and the Law* (New Delhi: Human Rights Network).

Quinn, G. and Degenner, T. (2002) *Human Rights and Disability* (United Nations, New York).

Raj, S.L.(1998) *Fifty Years after Freedom* (New Delhi: Indian Social Institute).

Shapiro, J.P. (1994) *No Pity* (New Delhi: Universal Law Publishing).

Stone, J.H. (Ed) (2005) *Culture and Disability: Providing Culturally Competent Services* (Thousand Oaks, CA: Sage).

Swain, J. et al (Eds) (1993) *Disabling Barriers Enabling Environments* (New Delhi: Sage Publications).

Thomson, R.G. (1997) *Extraordinary Bodies: Figuring Physical Disability in American Culture and Literature* (New York: Columbia University Press).

Verma, S.K. (Ed) (2002) *Rights of Persons with Disabilities* (New Delhi: Indian Law Institute).

MDS 006: Psycho-Social Aspects of Disability

This paper would examine the psychological theory and research pertaining to physical disability and persons with disabilities. Apart from examining the social attitudes regarding disability and the impact of disability on individual behavior, it also deals basically with the phenomena of blindness, deafness, orthopedic handicap, and epilepsy, and other disabling situations.

Suggested Readings

Albrecht, G. L. et al (Eds) (2001) *Handbook of Disability Studies* (Thousand Oaks, CA: Sage Publications).

--------(Eds) (2006) *Encyclopedia of Disability* (Thousand Oaks, CA: Sage Publications).

Asch, Adrienne and Mccarthy, Henry (n.d.) Infusing Disability Studies into Psychology Curriculum, available at: file:///C:/Users/sfd/Downloads/Infusing%20Disability%20Issues%20into%20Psychology.pdf

Dunn, Dana (2015) *The Social Psychology of Disability* (New York: OUP)

Dell Orto, A.E. and Power, P. W. (Eds) (2007) *The Psychological and Social Impact of Illness and Disablity* (New York: Springer Publishing Company), 5th edn.

Falvo, D. (2005) *Medical and Psychosocial Aspects of Chronic Illness and Disability*, 3rd edn., (Boston: Jones and Bartlett Publishers).

Karna, G.N. (1999) *The United Nations and Rights of Disabled Persons: A Study in Indian Perspective* (New Delhi: APH Pub. Co.).

King, R. et al (2007) *Handbook of Psychosocial Rehabilitation* (Blackwell Publishing).

Olkin, Rhoda and Pledger, Constance (2003) Can Disability Studies and Psychology join Hands, *American Psychologist*, 58 94), pp. 256-304.

Thomas, C. (2002) The 'Disabled Body, In: Mary Evans and Ellie Lee (Eds) *Real Bodies: A Sociological Introduction* (New York: Palgrave).

Shakespeare, T. (2006) *Disability Rights and Wrongs* (Oxon: Routledge).

Turner, D.M. and Stagg, K. (Eds) (2006) *Social Histories of Disability and Deformity* (Oxon: Routledge).

Vash, Carolyn L. and Crewe, Nancy M. (2003) *Psychology of Disability* (New York: Springer Publishing Company), second edition

Watermeyer, Brian (2013) *Towards a Contextual Psychology of Disablism* (London and New York: Routledge)

MDS 007: Disability, Assistive Devices and ICT

This paper would examine the best clinical practices and state-of-the-art Assistive Technology and Information/ Communication Technology devices, including the areas of Augmentative Communication, Cognitive Technologies, Computer Access, Environmental Control, Home Modification, Orthotics and Prosthetics, Seating and Wheeled Mobility, and Worksite Modification. Funding and Outcomes Measurement with respect to each area.

Suggested Readings

Adlam, T. et al (2004) The installation and support of internationally distributed equipment for people with dementia: *IEEE Transactions on Information Technology in Biomedicine*, 8 (3), pp. 253-257.

Bates, R. and Jones, M. (2003) Using Computer Software to Develop Switch Skills, *Technology and Persons with Disabilities,Conference Proceedings; retrieved at:* http://www.csun.edu/cod/conf/2003/proceedings/6.htm.

Behrmann, M. and Schaff, J. (2001) Assisting educators with assistive technology: Enabling children to achieve independence in living and learning, *Children and Families*, 42(3), pp. 24-28.

Bishop, J. (2003) The Internet for educating individuals with social impairments, *Journal of Computer Assisted Learning*, 19(4), pp. 546-556.

Bodine, Cathy (2013) *Assistive Technology and Science* (Los Angeles: Sage)

Cain, S. (2001) *Accessing Technology- Using Technology to Support the Learning and Employment Opportunities for Visually Impaired Users* (London: Royal National Institute for the Blind).

Cook, A. and Hussey, S. (2002) *Assistive Technologies- Principles and Practice*, 2nd Edition (Mosby).

Edwards, A.D.N. (Ed.) (1995) *Extra-Ordinary Human-Computer Interaction: Interfaces for Users with Disabilities*, Cambridge Series on Human-Computer Interaction (New York, Cambridge University Press), also available as part of the CD-rom, Overcoming Barriers: Theory and Practice in Disability, Cambridge University Press, 1999).

Franklin, K.S. (1991) Supported employment and assistive technology-A powerful partnership, In: S.L. Griffin and W.G. Revell (Eds) *Rehabilitation Counselor Desktop Guide to Supported Employment* (Richmond, VA: Virginia Commonwealth University Rehabilitation Research and Training Center on Supported Employment).

Gleeson, B. (2005) Can technology overcome the disabling city?, In: R. Butler and Hester Parr (Eds) (2005) *Mind and Body Space: Geographies of Illness, Impairment and Disability* (London and New York: Routledge).

Hawes, P. and Blenkhorn, P. (2002) Bridging the Gap between Aspiration and Capability for Aphasic and Brain Injured People, *Technology and Persons with Disabilities] Conference Proceedings; available at:* http://www.csun.edu/cod/conf/2002/proceedings/220.htm.

Lahm, E. and Morrissette, S. (1994) Zap 'em with assistive technology, Paper presented at the annual meeting of The Council for Exceptional Children, Denver, CO, April.

Lee, C. (1999) *Learning Disabilities and Assistive Technologies: An Emerging Way to Touch the Future* (Amherst, MA: McGowan Publications).

McKeown, S. (2000 *Unlocking Potential - How ICT can support children with special needs* (The Questions Publishing Company Ltd.).

Nisbet, P. and Poon, P. (1998) *Special Access Technology* (University of Edinburgh: The CALL Centre).

--------et al (1999) *Supportive Writing Technology* (University of Edinburgh: The CALL Centre).

Orpwood, R. (1990) Design methodology for aids for the disabled, *Journal of Medical Engineering Technology*, Jan-Feb; 14(1), pp. 2-10.

Poulson, D. et al (Eds) (1996) U*serfit: A Practical Handbook on User-centred Design for Assistive Technology* (TIDE USER Consortium).

Ravneberg, Bodil and Soderstrom, Sylvia (2017) *Disability, Society and Assistive Technology* (London and New York: Routledge)

Reddy, G.L. et al (1999) Assistive technology to overcome learning difficulties in children, *Journal of Disabilities and Impairments*, 13 (1 & 2).

--------(2006) Students with specific learning difficulties: detection and management, *Edutracks*, 6 (1), September.

Rose, D. and Meyer, A. (2000) Universal design for individual differences, *Educational Leadership*, 58(3), pp. 39-43.

Scherer, M. J. (2005) *Living in the State of Stuck: How Assistive Technology Impacts the Lives of People with Disabilities,* 4th Edition (Cambridge, MA: Brookline Books).

--------(2004) *Connecting to Learn: Educational and Assistive Technology for People with Disabilities*, Washington, DC: American Psychological Association (APA Books: ISBN 1-557-98982-6.

--------(Ed)(2002) *Assistive Technology: Matching Device and Consumer for Successful Rehabilitation* (Washington, DC: APA Books).

Van der Heijden, D. (2007) How Does Alternative Access to Computers Work?, June 26.

MDS 008: Disability, Education and Capacity Building

This course is structured so as to provide an overview of dis/ability within education. We will foreground historical, social, cultural and interpretive understandings of dis/ability, contrasting them with the medical, scientific, and psychological understandings of dis/ability within the context of schooling practices. Using personal narratives, media representations, contemporary research, historical accounts, legal and policy issues, the students would analyze competing claims of what dis/ability is. By analyzing multiple and interdisciplinary understandings of dis/ability from a wide variety of sources, they may be able to deepen their understanding of dis/ability issues within education and society. Thus, the students would be familiarized with the significance of special education, inclusive and general education for empowering and enhancing the capability of persons with disabilities.

Suggested Readings

Albrecht, G.L. et al (Eds) (2001) *Handbook of Disability Studies* (Thousand Oaks, CA: Sage Publications).

--------(Eds) (2006) *Encyclopedia of Disability* (Thousand Oaks, CA: Sage Publications).

Calderón-Almendros, Ignacio and Habegger-Lardoeyt, Sabina (2017) *Education, Disability and Inclusion: A Family Struggle against an Excluding School* (Rotterdam: Sense Publishers)

Crosling, G. et al (Eds) (2008) *Improving Student Retention in Higher Education* (London and New York: Routledge).

Danforth, S. and Gabel, S. L. (Eds) (2006) *Vital Questions facing Disability Studies in Education* (New York: Peter Lang).

Gabel, S. (Ed) (2005) *Disability Studies in Education: Readings in Theory and Method* (New York: Peter Lang).

Haines, Steve and Ruebain, David (Eds) (2011) *Education, Disability and Social Policy* (Bristol: Policy Press)

Heron, R. and Murray, B. (2003) *Assisting Disabled Persons in Finding Employment* (Bangkok: ILO East Asia Multidisciplinary Advisory Team/ILO Regional Office for Asia and the Pacific), 2nd edn.

Karna, G.N. (2001) *Disability Studies in India: Retrospects and Prospects* (New Delhi: Gyan Publishing House).

--------(1999) *The United Nations and the Rights of Disabled Persons: A Study in Indian Perspective* (New Delhi: APH Publishing Corporation).

Mishra, A.K. and R. Gupta (2006) Measurement of Disability-Disability Index: A Measure of Deprivation among Disabled, *Economic and Political Weekly*, 41 (38), pp. 4026-4029.

Mitra, S. and U. Sambamoorthi (2008) Disability and the Rural Labor Market in India: Evidence for Males in Tamil Nadu, *Economic and Political Weekly*, 36 (5), pp. 934-952.

--------(2006a) Measurement of Disability — Disability Estimates in India: What the Census and NSS Tell Us, *Economic and Political Weekly*, 41(38), pp. 4022-4025.

--------(2006b) Perspectives-Employment of Persons with Disabilities: Evidence from the National Sample Survey, *Economic and Political Weekly*, 41 (3), pp. 199-203.

Reddy, G.L. (2005) Special Education in Western Countries and India: A Comparative Study, *International Journal of Disability Studies*, 1 (1), pp.

--------(2007) Inclusive education: supportive systems for students with disabilities in higher education, *University News*, 45 (14).

--------et al (2009) Promoting inclusive schools: issues and practices, *International Educator*, 20 (1).

Rungta, S.K. (2004) Training and Employment of People with Disabilities: India 2002 (ILO), *GLADNET Collection*, Cornell University ILR School Year, retrieved at: http://digitalcommons.ilr.cornell.edu/cgi/viewcontent.cgi?article=1470&context=gladnetcollect Seale, J.K. (2006) *E-Learning and Disability in Higher Education: Accessibility Research and Practice* (London and New York: Routledge).

Snyder, S.L. and Mitchell, D.T. (2006) *Cultural Locations of Disability* (Chicago and London: The University of Chicago Press).

MDSP-2: Practicum – The theme and modality of the practicum shall be decided by the concerned teacher.

Semester-III

MDS 009: Disability, Society and Public Policy

This paper would examine the issue of development of public policy towards disability and equity issues within the Indian and international contexts, especially with regard to their impact on national, regional and local policies affecting persons with disabilities. The impact of grass roots organisations and activism are also included as an important area of study, looking at how disability advocacy has influenced the development of social policies at different times and places both historically and in contemporary society.

Suggested Readings

Albrecht, G.L. et al (Eds) (2001) *Handbook of Disability Studies* (Thousand Oaks, CA: Sage Publications).

--------(Eds) (2006) *Encyclopedia of Disability* (Thousand Oaks, CA: Sage Publications).

Barnes, C. (1992) *Disabling Imagery and the Media* (Halifax: Ryburn and British Council of Disabled People).

Barton, L. (Ed) (2005) *Disability and Dependency* (East Sussex: The Falmer Press).

Berkowitz, M. et al (1976) *Public Policy toward Disability* (New York: Preager).

--------and M. Anne Hill (Eds) (undated) *Disability and the Labour Market: Economic Problems, Policies and Programs* (Ithaca, NY: ILR Press).

Best, S. (2005) *Understanding Social Divisions* (London: Sage Publications Limited), especially Chapter 2.

Desai, A.N. (1995) *Helping the Handicapped* (New Delhi: Ashish Publishing House).

Hahn, Harlan (1985a) Disability Policy and the Problem of Discrimination, *American Behavioural Scientist*, 8, Jan.-Feb., pp. 293-318.

--------(1985b)Toward a Politics of Disability: Definitions, Disciplines, and Polices (Unpublished paper: Univ. of Southern California).

Hans, A. et al (Eds) (2003) *Women, Disability and Identity* (Sage Publication, New Delhi).

Hodges, J. (Ed) (1997) *Affirmative Action in the Employment of Ethnic Minorities and Persons with Disability* (Geneva: International Labour Office).

Goffman, E. (1963) *Stigma: Notes on the Management of Spoiled Identity* (New York: Touchstone).

Guffey, Elizabeth (2018) *Designing Disability: Symbols, Space, and Society* (London: Bloomsbury Academic)

Harriss-White, B. (1996) *The Political Economy of Disability and Development, with Special Reference to India,* UNRISD Discussion Paper, United Nations Research Institute for Social Development (Geneva).

Ingstad, B. and Whyte, S.R. (Eds) (1995) *Disability and Culture* (Berkeley: University of California Press).

Karna, G.N. (2001) *Disability Studies in India: Retrospects and Prospects* (New Delhi: Gyan Publishing House).

Kuppers, P. (2003) *Disability and Contemporary Performance: Bodies on Edge* (London and New York: Routledge).

Murickan, J. and Kareparamil, G. (1995) *Persons with Disabilities in Society* (Trivandrum: Kerala Federation of the Blind).

Swain, J. et al (Eds) (2003) *Controversial Issues in a Disabling Society* (Sheffield: Open University Press).

Titchkosky, Tanya (2006) *Disability, Self, and Society*(University of Toronto Press), rep.

Wilson, J.C. and Lewiecki-Wilson, C. (2001) *Embodied Rhetorics: Disability in Language and Culture* (Carbondale, IL:Southern Illinois Univ. Press).

Zola, I.K. (2003) *Missing Pieces: A Chronicle of Living with a Disability* (Philadelphia: Temple University Press).

MDS 010: Research Methodology in Disability Studies

This course is designed to explore current debates and issues on the implementation of disability research, including emphasis on emancipatory research and participant action research. Areas for discussion include an introduction to doing disability research, qualitative and quantitative research methodologies, involving persons with disabilities in policy and planning, assessment procedures, the dissemination of research findings and accessibility of information.

Suggested Readings

Altman, Barbara M.(Ed) *International Measurement of Disability Purpose, Method and Application* (Switzerland: Springer)

Barnes, C. and Mercer G. (1997) *Doing Disability Research* (Leeds: The Disability Press).

Baglieri, S. et al (2006) *Engaging in Disability Studies Research: An Autoethnographic Exploration,* presented at the American Educational Research Association's 2006 annual meeting at San Francisco, CA.

Beauchamp-Pryor, Karen et al (Eds) (2013) *Purpose, Process and Future Direction of Disability Research* (Rotterdam: Sense Publishers)

Brown, S.C. (2001) Methodological Paradigms that Shape Disability Research, In: Gary L. Albrecht et al (Eds) *Disability Studies Handbook.* (Thousand Oaks, CA: Sage), pp. 145-70.

Burns, R.B. (2000) *Introduction to Research Methods* (London: Sage).

Corker, M. and French, S. (Eds) (1999) *Disability Discourse* (Milton Keynes: Open University Press), pp. 129-35

Cresswell, J.A. (2002) *Research Design: Qualitative, Quantitative and Mixed Methods Approaches* (London, Sage publications).

Hartley, S. and Muhit, M. (2003) Guest Editorial: Using qualitative research methods for disability research in majority world countries, *Asia Pacific Disability Rehabilitation Journal,* 14 (2), pp. 103-14.

Kerschbaum, Stephanie L et al (Eds) (2017) *Negotiating Disability: Disclosure and Higher Education* (Ann Arbor: University of Michigan Press)

Mason, J. (2002) *Qualitative Researching* (London: Sage Publications), 2nd edn.

Morris, R.J. (Ed) (2008) *Disability Research and Policy: Current Perspectives* (New Jersey: Lawrence Erlbaum Associates Publishers).

Morris, Richard J. (2005) *Disability Research and Policy: Current Perspectives* (Mahwah NewJersey: Lawrence Erlbaum Associates Publishers)

Muecke, M. (1997) Policy as forethought in qualitative research. A paradigm from developing country social scientists, In: J. Morse (Ed) *Completing a qualitative project* (London, Sage publications).

Punch, K.F. (1998) *Introduction to Social Research: Quantitative and Qualitative Approaches* (London: Sage).

Rifkin, S. and Hartley, S. (1999) Teaching qualitative methods for disability research, *Saudi Journal of Disability and Rehabilitation*, 5 (1), pp. 7-15.

Rioux, M.H. (1997) When Myths Masquerade as Science: Disability Research from an Equality-Rights Perspective, In: Len Barton and Mike Oliver (Eds) *Disability Studies: Past, Present and Future* (Leeds: The Disability Press).

--------and Bach, M. (Eds) (1994) *Disability is not Measles: New Research Paradigms in Disability* (North York, Ont.: The Roeher Institute).

Shakespeare, Tom (Ed) (2015) *Disability Research Today: International Perspectives* (London and New York: Routledge)

--------(1996) Rules of engagement: doing disability research, *Disability and Society*, 11 (1), pp. 115-119.

Stone, E. and Priestly, M. (1996) *Parasites, pawns and partners: Disability research and the role of non-disabled researchers*, British Journal of Sociology, 47, pp. 699-716.

MDS 011: Disability, Family Support and Self Determination

This course is intended to highlight the role of teachers, professionals and social activists working in disability sector as also families supporting members with disabilities. The topics include the philosophy of family support and self-determination, cultural competence in supporting families, assessing needs and determining supports, identifying and coordinating resources, skills for working together with families and self- advocates, and evaluating family support programmes.

Suggested Readings

Annapurna, M. (1997) *Mentally Handicapped Children and Family Stress* (New Delhi: Discovery Publishing House).

Dell Orto, A. E. and Power, P. W. (Eds) (2007) *The Psychological and Social Impact of Illness and Disablity* (New York: Springer Pub. Co.), 5th edn.

--------and Marinelli, R. P. (Eds) (1995) *Encyclopedia of Disability and Rehabilitation* (Macmillan Library Reference USA).

Ferguson, P. M. (2001) Mapping the family: Disability Studies and the exploration of parental response to disability, In: Gary L. Albrecht et al (Eds) *Handbook of Disability Studies* (Thousand Oaks, CA: Sage), pp. 373-95.

Orr, R.J. (2003) *My Right to Play: A Child with Complex Needs* (Maidenhead: Open University Press).

Peate, I. and Fearns, D. (Eds) (2006) *Caring for People with Learning Disabilities* (West Sussex: John Wiley & Sons).

Prasher, V.P. and Janicki, M.P. (Eds) (2002) *Physical Health of Adults with Intellectual Disabilities* (Oxford: Blackwell Publishing Limited).

Reddy, G.L. et al (2005a) *Anti-Social Behaviour in Children: Detection and Management* (New Delhi: Discovery Publishing House).

--------et al (2005b) *Behaviour Disorders in Children: Identification, Assessment and Intervention Strategies* (New Delhi: Discovery Publishing House).

--------et al (2004) *Mental Retardation: Education and Rehabilitation Services* (New Delhi: Discovery Publishing House).

--------et al (2000) *Learning Disabilities: A Practical Guide to Practitioners* (New Delhi: Discovery Publishing House).

--------et al (2005) *Behaviour Disorder in Students: Detection and Management* (New Delhi: Discovery Publishing House).

Rimmerman, Arie (2015) *Family Policy and Disability* (Cambridge University Press).

Shah, S. (2010) Role of family in empowering the young disabled people, *International Journal of Disability Studies*, special issue on 'Disability Studies in Education: emerging issues', 4 (1 & 2), Jan.-Dec.

Shapiro, A. (1999) *Everybody Belongs: Changing Negative Attitudes toward Classmates with Disabilities* (New York: Routledge Falmer).

Titchkosky, T. (2003) *Disability, Self, and Society* (Toronto: Univ. of Toronto Press).

MDS 012: Disability, Sexuality and Independent Living

This course would give an insight to the rehabilitation professionals and others concerned for understanding the physiological and psychological aspects of human sexuality and the impact of disability and chronic illness on a person's sense of sexuality and sexual functioning. For people with disabilities, the everyday tasks of independent living can present unique challenges, but with sufficient assistance and social supports in place, these individuals can enjoy many of the same opportunities and control in their everyday lives that their able- bodied neighbors, family, and friends take for granted.

Suggested Readings

Balen, R. and Crawshaw (Eds) (2006) *Sexuality and Fertility Issues in Ill Health and Disability: From Early Adolescence to Adulthood* (London: Jessica Kingsley Publishers).

Barnes, C. (2000) A working social model? disability, work and disability politics in the 21st Century, *Critical Social Policy*, 20 (4), pp. 441-457.

Dell Orto, A. E. and Power, P. W. (Eds) (2007) *The Psychological and Social Impact of Illness and Disablity* (New York: Springer Pub. Co.), 5th edn.

---------and Marinelli, R. P. (Eds) (1995) *Encyclopedia of Disability and Rehabilitation* (Macmillan Library Reference USA).

Finger, A. (1990) *Past Due: A Story of Disability, Pregnancy and Birth* (London: The Women's Press).

Foucault, M. (1980) *The History of Sexuality, vol.1, An Introduction* (New York: Vintage).

---------1986) *The History of Sexuality, vol.2, The Use of Pleasure* (New York: Vintage).

---------(1988) *The History of Sexuality, vol.3, The Care of the Self* (New York: Vintage).

Gawali, G. (2007) Sexuality of women with disabilities: psycho- social issues, *International Journal of Disability Studies*, special issue on 'Disability, Sexuality and Hhuman Rights', 3 (1 & 2), Jan.-Dec., pp. 35-51.

Ghai, A. (2007) Some observations on sexual empowerment of disabled women in India, *International Journal of Disability Studies*, special issue on 'Disability, Sexuality and Human Rights', 3 (1 & 2), Jan.-Dec., pp. 26-34.

Griffin, L.K. (1996) *Informed Consent, Sexuality, and People with Developmental Disabilities: Strategies for Professional Decision-Making* (ARC Milwaukee).

International Journal of Disability Studies (2007) Special issue on 'Disability, Sexuality and Human Rights', 3 (1 & 2), Jan.- Dec., (New Delhi: Society for Disability and Rehabilitation Studies).

Kaufman, M. et al (2003) *Ultimate Guide to Sex and Disability California*: CLEIS).

Kempton, W. (1998) *Socialization and Sexuality: A Comprehensive Training Guide for Professionals Helping People with Disabilities That Hinder Learning* (Program Development Associates).

Kogut, J. and Vilardo, Susan (1993) *Teaching Persons with Mental Retardation about Sexuality and Relationships: An Instructional Guide* (Planned Parenthood of Connecticut).

Mackelprang, R.W. and Valentine, D. (Eds) (1996) *Sexuality and Disabilities: A Guide for Human Service Practitioners* (The Haworth Press, Inc.).

Mintz, S. (2007) *Unruly Bodies: Life Writings by Women with Disabilities* (Chapel Hill: University of North Carolina).

Morris, J. (1989) *Abled Lives: Women's Experiences of Paralysis* (London: The Women's Press).

--------(1991) *Pride against Prejudice: A Personal Politics of Disability* London: The Women's Press).

Neistadt, M. E. and Freda, M. (1987) *Choices: A Guide to Sex Counseling with Physically Disabled Adults,* illustrated by Kerry Anne O'Reilly (Krieger Publishing Company).

Olsen, R. and Clarke, H. (2003) *Parenting and Disability: Disabled Parents' Experiences of Raising Children* (Bristol: The Polity Press).

Parker, G. (1993) *With this Body: Caring and Disability in Marriage* (Buckingham: University Press).

Perlin, Michael L. and Lynch, Alison J. (2016) *Sexuality, Disability, and the Law: Beyond the Last Frontier?* (Houndmills: Palgrave Macmillan)

Reddy, G.L. and Poornima, R. (2007) Disability and sexuality: a special education perspectives, *International Journal of Disability Studies*, 3 (1 & 2).

--------(2008) Disability and sexuality: teaching and research perspectives, *International Journal of Disability Studies*, 4 (1 & 2).

Sandowski, Carol L. (1989) *Sexual Concerns When Illness or Disability Strikes* (Charles C. Thomas Publisher, Ltd.).

Schover, L.R. (1988) *Sexuality and Chronic Illness: A Comprehensive Approach* (Guilford Publications).

Shakespeare, T. (1996) *Disability, Identity and Difference*, in: Colin Barnes and Geof Mercer (Eds) *Exploring the Divide: Illness and Disability* (Leeds: The Disability Press).

--------et al (Eds) (1996) *The Sexual Politics of Disability: Untold Desires* (Leeds: The Disability Press).

--------et al (2001) *Making the Difference: disability, politics, recognition*, in: Gary A. Albrecht et al (Eds) *Handbook of Disability Studies* (Thousand Oaks: Sage), pp. 546-564.

Shildrick, Margrit (2009) *Dangerous Discourses of Disability, Subjectivity and Sexuality* (Houndmills: Palgrave Macmillan)

Sipski, M.L. and Alexander, C. J. (1997) *Sexual Function in People with Disability and Chronic Illness: A Health Professional's Guide* (Aspen Publishers Inc.).

MDS 013: Disability and Civil Rights Movement

This course would provide an overview and analysis of various civil rights movements as also the disability rights movement in the global and Indian contexts and the social changes that have resulted from these movements. An attempt is also made to establish linkages between civil rights and disability rights movement. It would also examine the historical development of global disability rights movement as a social movement and its impact on policy formulations for empowering the persons with disabilities.

Suggested Readings

Beckett, A.E. (2006) *Citizenship and Vulnerability: Disability and Issues of Social and Political Engagement* (Houndmills: Palgrave Macmillan).

Couser, G.T. (1997) *Recovering Bodies: Illness, Disability, and Life Writing* (Madison, WI: University of Wisconsin Press).

Fleischer, D.J. and Zames, F. (2001) *The Disability Rights Movement: From Charity to Confrontation* (Philadelphia: Temple University Press).

Karna, G.N. (2000d) Disability rights movement: conceptual framework and its implications for India, *Disabilities and Impairments*, 14(1), 15-22.

McNeese, Tim (2013) *Disability Rights Movement* (Minneapolis: ABDO Publishing Company)

O' Brien, R. (Ed) (2004) *Voices from the Edge* (Oxford University Press).

Riddell, S. (1999) *Disability and Civil Rights in the New Millennium* (University of Glasgow: Strathclyde Centre for Disability Research).

Scotch, R. (2001) *From Good Will to Civil Rights: Transforming Federal Disability Policy* (Philadelphia: Temple University Press).

Shapiro, J.P. (1993) *No Pity: People with Disabilities Forging a New Civil Rights Movement* (New York: Times Books).

Stroman, D.F. (2003) *The Disability Rights Movement: From Deinstitutionalization to Self-determination* (Lanham, MD: University Press of America, Inc).

MDS 014: Disability and Special/Inclusive Education

This course gives insight to the teachers, special educators as also para- professionals and school administrators about the ways and means of facilitating barrier - free physical, social, psychological, educational learning environments to the pupil with special needs. The topics to be covered are the philosophy behind inclusive education, need for restructuring the organizational set- up of schools, the innovative teaching-learning methodologies to accommodate diverse learners with various disabilities, need for application of adoptive as also information and communication technologies to augment the learning of pupil with special needs, identification, assessment and differential educational evaluation procedures for children with special needs.

Suggested Reading

Adams, M. and Brown, S. (Eds)(2006) *Towards Inclusive Learning in Higher Education: Developing Curricula for Disabled Students* (Oxon: Routledge).

Ahmad Hassanein, Elsayed Elshabrawy (2015) *Inclusion, Disability and Culture* (Rotterdam: Sense Publishers)

Armstrong, F. and Barton, L. (Eds) (2000) *Disability, Human Rights, and Education: Cross-Cultural Perspectives* (Sheffield, UK: Open University Press).

Barton, L. and Armstrong, F. (Eds) (2008) *Policy, Experience and Change: Cross-Cultural Reflections on Inclusive Education* (London: Springer).

Drifte, C. (2004) *Encouraging Positive Behaviour in the Early Years: A Practical Guide* (London: Paul Chapman Publishing).

Hallahan, D.P. and Koffman, J. M. (1991) *Exceptional Children: Introduction to Special Education* (London: Prentice Hall).

International Journal of Disability Studies (2010) Special issue on 'Disability Studies in Education', 4 (1 & 2), Jan.-December (New Delhi: Society for Disability and Rehabilitation Studies).

Kirk, S.A. et al (2006) *Educating Exceptional Children* (Houghton Miffin, USA).

Kluth, P. et al (Eds) (n.d.) *Access to Academics for All Students: Critical Approaches to Inclusive Curriculum, Instruction, and Policy* (New Jersey: Lawrence Erlbaum Associates, Publishers).

Mercer, C.D. (1997) *Students with Learning Disabilities* (New Jersey: Merril Prentice Hall).

Rao, L. Govinda et al (2005) *Status of Education of Children with Disabilities* (Secunderabad: NIMH).

Reddy, G.L. et al (2006) *Children with Disabilities: Awareness, Attitude and Competencies of Teachers* (New Delhi: Discovery Publishing House).

--------(2007) *Occupational Stress, Professional Burn out and Job Satisfaction of Special Education Teachers* (New Delhi: Discovery Publishing House).

--------et al (2003) *Education of Children with Special Needs* (New Delhi: Discovery Publishing House).

--------et al (2004) *Mental Retardation: Education and Rehabilitation Services* (New Delhi: Discovery Publishing House).

--------et al (2000) *Learning Disabilities: A Practical Guide to the Practitioners* (New Delhi: Discovery Publishing House).

--------et al (2004) *Hearing Impairment: An Educational Consideration* (New Delhi: Discovery Publishing House).

Gallagher, D.J. et al (2004) *Challenging Orthodoxy in Special Education: Dissenting Voices* (Denver: Love Publishing Company).

Minow, M. (1990) *Making all the Difference: Inclusion, Exclusion, and American Law* (Ithaca, NY: Cornell University Press).

Osgood, R.L. (2008) *The History of Special Education: A Struggle for Equality in American Public Schools* (London: Praeger).

Sen, Amartya (n. d.) Disability and justice, retrieved at: http://72.14.235.132/search?q=cache: gNVnh8e09NgJ: siteresources.worldbank.org/DISABILITY/214576-1092421729901/20291152/Amartya_Sen_ Speech. doc+ Amartya+ Sen +disability & hl =e n&ct= clnk &cd =1 & gl=in

Sen, Amartya and J.D. Wolfensohn (2004) Helping disabled people out of the shadows, *The Korea Times*, 21 December, retrieved at: http://tinyurl.com/4vbzhw (accessed 15 September 2008).

Sen, Anima (1992) *Mental Handicap among Rural Indian Children (New Delhi:* Sage Publications).

Sharma, Umesh (2005) Integrated Education in India: Challenges and Prospects, *Disability Studies Quarterly*, 25 (1), available at: www.dsq-sds.org

Singhal, Nidhi (2008) *Forgotten Youth: Disability and Development in India* (Cambridge: Research Consortium on Educational Outcomes and Poverty), retrieved at: http://recoup.educ.cam.ac.uk/publications/WP14-NS.pdf

Verma, G.K. et al (Eds) (2007) *International Perspectives on Educational Diversity and Inclusion: Studies from America, Europe and India* (Oxon: Routledge).

World Bank (2007) *People with Disabilities in India: From Commitments to Outcomes* (New Delhi).

MDS 015: Disability and Public Transportation

This course is basically designed so as to get the students familiarized with the mobility needs for persons with disabilities within and outside the local communities. The topics include the ways and means of including the excluded population in providing basic amenities like public transportation and accessible environments for facilitating independent living, architectural and structural designing of buildings, roads, vehicles (buses, trains, aeroplanes etc.) for road, rail, air and ship services, installing appropriate signals/ signages at stop overs, arrival and departure terminals, critical evaluation of existing facilities, policies and programmes for barrier- free environments, and research and innovations for enhancing mobility and independence of persons with various disabilities.

Suggested Readings

Alvarez, Eduardo (undated) Pathways to Accessibility: Disability and the Physical Environment in Latin America and the Caribbean; available at: http://www.iadb.org/sds/doc/Rev2 bEdited Disability %2 D Infrastructure Alvarez.pdf

Benson, B.L. et al (1981) *Solutions for problems of visually-impaired users of rail rapid transit. Volume 1 of: Improving communications with the visually impaired in rail rapid transit systems* (Washington, DC: U.S. Department of Transportation).

Brail, R., Hughes, J. and Arthur, C. (1976) *Transportation Services for the Disabled and Elderly* (New Brunswick, NJ: Center for Urban Policy and Research).

Bucks, Christa (Ed) (1997) *A World of Options: A Guide to International Exchange, Travel, and Community Service for Persons with Disabilities,* 3d ed. (Eugene, OR: Mobility International).

Chew, K.A., and Manzer, D. (1986) Light rail or light rapid transit in Western Canada: A lesson planning aid, paper presented at the International Conference on the Visually Impaired Traveller in Mass Transit - Issues in Orientation and Mobility.

Corn, A., and Zachs, S.Z. (1994) The impact of non-driving on adults with visual impairments, *Journal of Vision Impairment and Blindness,* Jan-Feb, pp. 53-68.

Fischer, G., & Sullivan, J. (2002) Human-Centered Public Transportation Systems for Persons with Cognitive Disabilities - Challenges and Insights for Participatory

Design, a paper presented at the Participatory Design Conference (PDC'02), Malmö University, Sweden; available: http://www.cs.colorado.edu/~l3d/clever/assets/pdf/gf-pdc2002-mfa.pdf]

Gärling, T. et al (1994) Computational-process modelling of household activity scheduling, *Transportation Research* (n.p.).

Golledge, R. G. et al (1995) Public Transit Use by Non-Driving Disabled Persons: the Case of the Blind and Vision Impaired, paper prepared for the Annual PATH Conference, Richmond Field Station, October 13; available at: http://www.path.berkeley.edu/path/publications/pdf/PWP/96/PWP-96-01.pdf

--------et al (1991) Designing a personal guidance system to aid navigation without sight: Progress on the GIS component, *International Journal of Geographical Information Systems*, 5, pp. 373-396.

--------et al (1994) Auditory maps as alternatives to tactual maps, paper presented at the 4th International Symposium on Maps and Graphics for the Visually Impaired, São Paulo, Brazil, February 20-26.

Hunter-Zaworski, K. (1994) *Accessing Public Transportation: New Technologies Aid Persons with Sensory or Cognitive Disabilities* (Washington, DC: Transportation Research Board).

ILO (2002) Managing disability in the workplace; available at: http://www.ilo.org/public/english/employment/skills/disability/download/code.pdf

Imrie, R. (1996) *Disability and the City: International Perspectives* (London: Paul Chapman Publishing Ltd.).

Klatzky, R.L. et al (1990) Acquisition of route and survey knowledge in the absence of vision, *Journal of Motor Behavior*, 22, 1, pp. 19-43.

Loomis, J.M. et al (1993) Personal guidance system for the visually impaired using GPS, GIS, and VR technologies, paper presented at the Conference on Virtual Reality and Persons with Disabilities, San Francisco, California, June 17-18.

O' Brien, R. (Ed) (2004) *Voices from the Edge* (Oxford University Press).

Pfeiffer, D. (1990) Public Transit Access for Disabled Persons in the United States, *Disability & Society*, 5 (2), pp. 153-66.

Steinfeld, E. (1977) Major Issues in Developing Building Standards, In: Michael Bednars (Ed) *Barrier-Free Environments* (Stroudsburg, PA: Dowden, Hutchinson and Ross).

Svenson, K. (1994) The use of light rail or light rapid transit systems by individuals with severe visual impairment, *Journal of Vision Impairment and Blindness*, Jan-Feb.

Welsh, R.L. and Blasch, B.B. (1980) *Foundations of orientation and mobility* (New York: American Foundation for the Blind).

Wijk, M. (1990) *European Manual for an Accessible Built Environment* (Utrecht: IG-Nederland).

MDSP-3: Internship Programme

The internship programme of 15 days' duration in special schools or inclusive schools to gain the first hand experience about the inclusive/special education provisions and practices, teaching and learning methodologies followed for promoting inclusive schools and communities for pupil with diverse needs. After the successful completion of the period, the students shall submit a brief report testified by the head of the institution.

Semester-IV

MDS 016: Dissertation Work

Students could select any topic of contemporary relevance in Disability Studies for Dissertation in consultation with their mentor/supervisor. Through the dissertation, the students could demonstrate their ability to develop and complete an in-depth analysis, select and use of appropriate research methods, deploy advanced theoretical concepts and relate a focused study to broaden the contemporary debates in the field of Disability Studies.

MDS 017: Politics of Inclusion and Exclusion: A Study of Laws and Policies

The current topics relevant to inclusion and exclusion with special reference to Indian contexts will be reviewed in this course. Contemporary influences related to ethics, political, social, economic impacts of the policies and programmes will be analysed. The ethical underpinnings of different legislations, statutes, policy and service delivery will be examined. This course will seek to examine the ethical dilemmas in the community that provide the foundation for activism. A critical analysis of research in this respect will give an opportunity to the students to gain understanding about the constitutional and legislations as also policy and ethical frameworks guiding right actions.

Suggested Readings

Alur, M. and Rioux, M. (2000) *Included: An exploration of six early education pilot projects for children with disabilities in India* (New Delhi: UNICEF, South Asia Regional Office, India).

Bickenbach, J. (2001) Disability human rights law and policy, In G.L. Albrecht et al (Eds) *Handbook of Disability Studies* (Thousand Oaks, California: Sage Publications).

Gleeson, B. (1999) *Geographies of Disability* (New York: Routledge).

Government of India (n.d.) *Constitution of India*, especially Part-III & IV (New Delhi: Ministry of Law, Justice and Company Affairs).

--------(2016) *Rights of Persons with Disabilities Act* (New Delhi: Ministry of Law & Justice).

--------(1992) *Rehabilitation Council of India Act* (New Delhi: Ministry of Law, Justice & Company Affairs).

--------(1999) *National Trust for Persons with Autism, Cerebral Palsy and Multiple Disabilities Act* (New Delhi: Ministry of Law, Justice & Company Affairs).

--------(2013) Mental Health Act (New Delhi: Ministry of Law & Justice), initially enacted in 1987.

Kessel, Martina and Merziger, Patrick (Eds) (2012) *The Politics of Humour: Laughter, Inclusion, and Exclusion in the Twentieth Century* (University of Toronto Press)

Mitchell, D.T. and Snyder, S. L. (2003) *Narrative Prosthesis: Disability and the Dependencies of Discourse* (Ann Arbor: University of Michigan Press).

Mitra, S. (2006) The capability approach and disability, *Journal of Disability Policy Studies*, 16 (4), pp. 236-247.

Norwich, B. (2008) *Dilemmas of Difference, Inclusion and Disability: International Perspectives and Future Directions* (Oxon: Routledge).

O' Brien, R. (Ed) (2004) *Voices from the Edge* (Oxford University Press).

Quinn, G. and Degener, T. (2002) *Human Rights and Disability* (New York: United Nations).

Rajalakshmi, K. (2002) Social Issues: A Law on Paper, *The Frontline*, 19 (7), Mar. 30 - April 12.

Titchkosky, T. (2007) *Reading & Writing Disability Differently: The Textured Life of Embodiment* (Toronto: University of Toronto Press).

Reddy, G.L. (2009) Education, research and innovations for inclusive societies, in: Souvenir of the International Conference, held at School of Education & HRD, Dravidian University, Kuppam (AP), March.

United Nations (2006) *United Nations Convention on Rights of Persons with Disabilities* (New York: United Nations).

--------(2007) From *Exclusion to Equality: Realizing the Rights of Persons with Disabilities*, Handbook for Parliamentarians on the Convention on the Rights of Persons with Disabilities and its Optional Protocol (Geneva).

Ware, L. (2004) *Ideology and the Politics of (In)Exclusion* (New York: Peter Lang).

MDS 018: Disability Management and Rehabilitation Technology

This course will provide a comprehensive overview of the principles and practices of disability management in the workplace. The course begins with an introduction to the interdisciplinary nature of return to work services and interventions, theoretical foundations of disability management and benchmark models or approaches used, and the typical issues and needs among persons challenged by TRW barriers. The application of management skills in resolving disability management problems will also be covered including traditional management skills in the areas of budgeting, human resources, service provision and problem-solving skills.

Suggested Readings

Anderberg, P. (2006) FACE: Disabled People, Technology and Internet (Lund University: Division of Rehabilitation Engineering Research/Deptt. of Design Sciences), Doctoral Thesis CERTEC: LTH, No. 1.

Bright, K. and Giulio, R. D. (undated) *Inclusive Buildings: Designing and Managing Accessible Environments* (Blackwell Science).

Federici, Stefano and Scherer, Marcia Joslyn (2018) *Assistive Technology Assessment Handbook* (New York: CRC Press), second edition.

Friedman, H.S. (Ed) (2001) *The Disorders: Specialty Articles from the Encyclopedia of Mental Health* (San Diego: Academic Press).

Guha, S.K. (2000) Rehabilitation of the disabled: Technological support, *International Journal of Disability Studies*, special inaugural issue, Oct. - Dec., pp.41-48.

Harrington, C. (2005) *Barrier- Free Travel: A Nuts and Bolts Guide for Wheelers and Slow Walkers—The Definitive Guide to Accessible Travel*, 2nd edn. (New York: Demos Medical Publishing).

Helal, A.S. et al (Eds) (2008) *The Engineering Handbook of Smart Technology for Aging, Disability and Independence* (New Jersey: John Wiley & Sons).

Lerner, N. and Straus, J.N. (Eds) (2006) *Sounding Off: Theorizing Disability in Music* (New York: Routledge).

Manduchi, Roberto and Sri Kurniawan (2012) *Assistive Technology for Blindness and Low Vision* (Boca Raton: CRC Press)

Nitnaware, R.C. (2006) *Home Instructions on Physiotherapy in the field of Mental Retardation* (Secunderabad: NIMH).

Priestley, M. (2003) *Disability: A Life Course Approach* (Cambridge: Polity Press).

Reddy, G.L. et al (2005) *Anti-Social Behaviour in Children: Detection and Management* (New Delhi: Discovery Publishing House).

--------et al (2005) *Behaviour Disorders in Children: Identification, Assessment and Intervention Strategies* (New Delhi: Discovery Publishing House).

Wassreman, D. et al (Eds) (2005) *Quality of Life and Human Difference* (Cambridge University Press).

MDS 019: Aging and Disability

This course studies individuals who are either chronologically older or who may be experiencing functional changes typical of older persons. Since some individuals, suffering from Down's Syndrome or Cerebral Palsy may experience changes typical of the aging process as early as 25 years of age, it is essential to cover this aspect in core courses on Disability Studies. This course identifies strategies for supports for families, friends, service providers, organizations, and members of the community to improve the lives of older persons. Topics include the aging process, a paradigm for dementia care, specific medical concerns, community membership, community building, team building, decision making, and family supports.

Suggested Readings

Albrecht, G.L. et al (Eds) (2001) *Handbook of Disability Studies* (Thousand Oaks, CA: Sage Publications).

--------(Eds) (2006) *Encyclopedia of Disability* (Thousand Oaks, CA: Sage Publications).

Becker, G. (1994) The Oldest Old: Autonomy in the Face of Frailty, *Journal of Aging Studies* 8(1), pp. 59-76.

Bortz, W. M. (2002) A Conceptual Framework of Frailty: A Review, *Journals of Gerontology Series A: Biological Sciences and Medical Sciences*,57a (5), pp. 283-289.

Chater, K. (2002) Aging: A Body of Resistance, *Nursing and Health Sciences,* 4(3), pp. 123-130.

Dowling, C. (2000) *The Frailty Myth: Women Approaching Physical Equality* (New York: Random House).

Ebersole, P. et al (2004) *Toward Healthy Aging: Human Needs & Nursing Response,* 6th edn. (St. Louis, MO: C.V. Mosby).

Gitlin, L. (1995) Why Older People Accept or Reject Assistive Technology, *Generations* (Spring), pp. 41-46.

Hammel, J. and Nochajski, S. (Eds) (2001) *Aging and Developmental Disability: Current Research, Programming, and Practice Implications* (Binghamton, NY: Haworth).

Helal, Abdelsalam et al (Eds) (2008) *The Engineering Handbook of Smart Technology for Aging, Disability and Independence* (Wiley)

Helal, A. et al (2008) *The Engineering Handbook of Smart Technology for Aging, Disability, and Independence* (London and New York: Wiley).

Heller, T. and Marks, B. (2006) Aging, In: Gary L. Albrecht et al (Eds) *Encyclopedia of Disability, vol. 1* (Thousand Oaks, CA: Sage Publications), pp. 67-78.

Herr, S. and Weber, G. (Eds) (1998) *Aging, Rights, and Quality of Life* (Baltimore: Paul H. Brookes).

Janicki, M. and Ansello, E. (Eds) (2000) *Community Supports for Aging Adults with Lifelong Disabilities* (Baltimore: Paul H. Brookes).

Janicki, M.P. and Dalton, A.J. (Eds) (1998) *Dementia and Aging Adults with Intellectual Disabilities: A Handbook* (Philadelphia: Francis and Taylor).

Kemp, B.J. and Mosqueda, L. (2004) *Aging with a Disability: What the Clinician Needs to Know* (Baltimore: Johns Hopkins University Press).

Kennedy, J. (Ed) (2003) *Journal of Disability Policy Studies*, Special Issue on Disability and Aging, 12(4).

Rimmer, J.H. et al (2004) Improvements in Physical Fitness in Adults with Down Syndrome, *American Journal on Mental Retardation*,109(2),pp.165–174.

MDS 020: Women, Disability and Discrimination

The voice of women in multiple minority status issues is largely missing from discussions of disability. This course examines the meaning and experience of being female and disabled and/or a cultural/ethnic minority member. An in-depth examination of the intersection of sex-roles stereotypes, disability stereotypes, and cultural stereotypes occurs through readings, interviews, and research

Suggested Readings

Cooper, M. (1990) *Women and Disability* (Canberra: Disabled People's International).

Fawcett, B. (2000) *Feminist Perspectives on Disability* (Essex: Pearson Education Limited).

Fine, M. and Asch, A. (1988) *Women with Disabilities: Essays in Psychology, Culture, and Politics* (Philadelphia: Temple University Press).

Frank, G. (2000) *Venus on Wheels: Two Decades of Dialogue on Disability, Biography and Being Female in America* (Berkeley and Los Angeles, California: University of California Press).

Garland-Thomson, R. (1994) Redrawing the boundaries of feminist Disability Studies, *Feminist Disability Studies*, 20(3), 583-597.

Ghai, A. (2007) *(Dis)embodied Form: Issues of Disabled Women* (New Delhi: Har Anand Publications).

--------(2002) Disabled women: An excluded agenda of Indian feminism, *Hypatia*, 17(3), pp. 49-66.

Hales, G. (Ed)(1996) *Beyond Disability: Towards an Enabling Society* (Thousand Oaks, CA: Sage Publications).

Ghosh, A. (2007) Women with disabilities and sexual and Reproductive health with special reference to HIV/AIDS, *International Journal of Disability Studies*, special issue on 'disability, sexuality and human rights', 3 (1 & 2), Jan.- Dec., pp. 52-68.

Hans, A. et al (Eds) (2003) *Women, Disability and Identity* (New Delhi: Sage Publication).

Hillyer, B. (1993) *Feminism and Disability* (Norman, OK: University of Oklahoma Press).

Hubbard, R. (1997) Abortion and disability: Who should and should not inhabit the world, In: L. Davis (Ed) *The Disability Studies Reader* (New York: Routledge), pp. 187-202.

Keith, L. (Ed) (1994) *Mustn't grumble: Writings by Disabled Women* (London: The Women's Press).

Lonsdale, S. (1990) *Women and Disability* (New York: St. Martin's Press).

Morris, J. (1993) Feminism and disability, *Feminist Review*, 43, pp. 57-70.

Morris, J. (1992) Personal and political: A feminist perspective on researching physical disability, *Disability, Handicap & Society*, 7 (2), pp. 157-166.

Morris, J. (1998) *Pride against prejudice: Transforming Attitudes to Disabilities*, rep. (North Pomfret, VT: Trafalgar Square).

Frank, G. (2000) *Venus on Wheels: Two decades of dialogue on disability, biography, and being female in America* (Berkeley: University of California Press).

Kittay, E. et al (Eds)(2001) Special issue: Feminism and Disability, *Hypatia*, 16(4).

Monro, S. (2005) *Gender Politics* (London: Pluto Press).

Pearman, Tory Vandeventer (2010) *Women and Disability in Medieval Literature* (New York: Palgrave Macmillan)

Rogers, J. (2006) *The Disabled Women's Guide to Pregnancy and Birth* (New York: Demos Medical Publishers).

Saxton, M. and Howe, F. (Eds) (1993) *With Wings: An Anthology of Literature by and about Women with Disabilities* (New York: Feminist Press at the City University of New York).

Smith, Julia L.T. (2015) *Women, Disability and Mental Distress* (Surrey: Ashgate Publishing Limited)

Tremain, S. (Ed) (1999) *Bodies of Knowledge: Critical Perspectives on Disablement and Disabled Women* (Toronto: Women's Press).

Wendell, S. (1996) *The Rejected Body: Feminist Philosophical Reflections on Disability* (New York: Routledge).

Willmuth, M. and Holcomb, L. (1994) *Women with Disabilities: Found V*oices (Binghamton, NY: The Haworth Press, Inc).

MDS 021: Guidance and Counselling in Disability Studies

This course is designed to motivate the students for developing graduate skills, subject expertise and exploration of a range of learning opportunities which will subsequently enable them to make an informed choice when determining potential future career pathways. The part routes of the programme encourage students to acquire knowledge and insight into their chosen subjects, related disciplines, professions, organisations and agencies. Students will develop skills in communication, self-management, reflection, critical analysis, discussion and evaluation and have opportunities to focus on topics which interest them. They will, thus, also gain insight into a range of theoretical frameworks that underpin their chosen subject, developing an appreciation and understanding of contemporary ways of working in a range of different contexts.

Suggested Readings

Blustein, D.L. (2006) *The Psychology of Working* (Mahwah, NJ: Lawrence Erlbaum Associates Publishers).

Charema, J. and Ngazimbi, E. E. (undated) The Approaches used in Counseling Parents of Children with Disabilities in the Western and African Tradition With Particular Emphasis to Zimbabwe, available at: http://www.ohiocounseling.org/docs/JA/John_Charema_Ohio_Final_4-05-09.pdf

Bond, T. (2008) *Standards and Ethics for Counselling in Action* (London: Sage Publications).

Corey, G. (2001) *Theory and Practice of Counselling and Psychotherapy*, 6th edn. (Pacific Grove, Brooks Cole).

Dryden, W. and Reeves, A. (2008) *Key Issues for Counselling in Action* (London: Sage Publications).

Gilliland, J. and Bowman (2003) *Theories and Strategies in Counseling and Psychotherapy*, 5th ed. (Boston: Allyn and Bacon).

McLeod, J. (2009) *An Introduction to Counselling*, 4th edn. (Maidenhead: Open University Press).

McLeod, J. (2009) *An Introduction to Counselling*, 4th edn. (Maidenhead: Open University Press).

Milner, J. and O'Byrne, P. (2002) *Brief Counselling: Narratives and Solutions* (Basingstoke: Palgrave).

MPhil/PhD in Disability Studies

MPhil in Disability Studies (MPDS)

The degree of MPhil in Disability Studies shall have the status of an intermediate Degree between the first Post-Graduate Degree (i.e. MA/MSc) and the Doctorate Degree. It will have combination of course work, field work and research components and will give the student adequate background for advanced research. The students pursuing this course will have to submit Dissertation in partial fulfillment of requirements for the award of MPhil degree.

The submitted Dissertation will have to be evaluated by one external examiner and the internal assessment by supervisor. The MPhil programme to be launched by any Centre or Department of Disability Studies would be the first such degree of its kind in the area of Disability Studies anywhere in the world.

Eligibility

Candidates with Master's Degree in Disability Studies, Rehabilitation Sciences, Special Education/Education or any streams of humanities and social sciences with at least 55% marks; or Master's Degree in Natural, Biological/Medical Sciences, Engineering or Management Sciences with at least 60% marks, are eligible to apply for admission to MPhil/PhD programme of studies.

MPhil Degree Requirements

*Minimum Credit requirements= 24 (Duration: 4 semesters; CGPA requirements 7.0)

In order to be qualified to get the degree of MPhil/PhD in Disability Studies, the student will have to secure 24 Credits in all—including the course work (12 Credits), during the course of two semesters with prescription of 2 credits for seminar, 10 credits for dissertation (the break- up being 8 credits for dissertation preparation and 2 credits for viva-vice). However, the student will have the option to join PhD directly after completing one year course work of 12 credits with minimum score of grade 'A minus' (7 points).

The first year (comprising two semesters of 6 months' duration each) of the programme would have 12 credits. Each course carries 3 credits and dissertation work of 10 Credits (the break-up being 8 credits for dissertation and 2 credits for viva-voce). The course titles and required credits are given semester-wise hereunder:

Courses

First Year: Semester-I

- MPDS 001: Contemporary Theories of Disability Studies (3 Credits)

- MPDS 002: The Sociology of Disability and Rehabilitation (3 Credits)

First Year: Semester-II

- MPDS 003: Disability, Human Rights Law and Public Policy (3 Credits)
- MPDS 004: Advanced Research Methodology and Statistical Techniques in Disability Studies (3 Credits)

Second Year: Semester-III & IV

- MPDS 005: Research Colloquium and Seminar on the chosen area for research work for MPhil programme (2 credits)
- MPDS 006: Dissertation Work (10 Credits)—8 credits for dissertation preparation and 2 credits for viva-voce
- MPDS 001: Contemporary Theories of Disability Studies

This course is designed to give the students opportunity to critically evaluate recent theoretical debates and developments within the interdisciplinary field of Disability Studies. Apart from addressing the positivist, interpretative and 'emancipatory' methodologies, alongside associated data collection and analytical strategies, the scholars will also examine their significance for disability research. Thus, they will get the opportunity of gaining an in- depth understanding and knowledge about theoretical perspectives, the various definitions and approaches to impairment and disability, and disability as an equal opportunities and policy issues. Not only that they will explore the impact of myths and prejudices, industrialization and the welfare state upon cultural representations of disability.

Suggested Readings

Albrecht, G.L. et al (Eds) (2001) *Handbook of Disability Studies* (Thousand Oaks, California: Sage Publications).

--------(Eds) (2006) *Encyclopedia of Disability* (Thousand Oaks, California: Sage Publications).

Altman, B.M. and Barnartt, S.N. (Eds) (2006) *International Views on Disability Measures: Moving toward Comparative Measurement*, Research in Social Science and Disability, Vol. 4 (Oxford: Elsevier).

Barnes, C. and Mercer, G. (Eds) (2002) *Disability Studies Today* (Cambridge: Polity Press).

--------et al (Eds) (1999) *Exploring Disability: A Sociological Introduction* (Cambridge: Polity Press).

Barnes, Elizabeth (Ed) (2016) *The Minority Body : A Theory of Disability* (OUP)

Barton, L. and Oliver, M. (Eds) (1997) *Disability Studies: Past, Present and Future* (Leeds: The Disability Press).

Corker, M. and Shakespeare, T. (Eds) (2002) *Disability/ Postmodernity: Embodying Disability Theory* (New York: Continuum).

Danforth, S. and Gabel, S. L. (Eds) (2006) *Vital Questions facing Disability Studies in Education* (New York: Peter Lang).

Davis, Lennard J. (2014) *The Disability Studies Reader* (New York and London: Routledge), fourth edition

Davis, L.J. (2002) *Bending over backwards: Disability, Dismodernism and other Difficult Positions* (New York: NYU Press).

Goodley, Dan et al (Eds) (2012) *Disability and Social Theory: New Developments and Directions* (New York: Palgrave Macmillan)

Green, D. and Meekosha, H. (2004) *Disability Studies in Australian Universities* (Sydney: Disability Studies and Research Institute and School of Social Work, University of New South Wales).

Karna, G.N. (2001) *Disability Studies in India: Retrospects and Prospects* (New Delhi: Gyan Publishing House).

--------(2007) Disability studies in India: new directions for future, Disability Studies in Higher Education: Monograph Series No. 2 (New Delhi: Society for Disability and Rehabilitation Studies).

Kasnitz, D. and Shuttleworth, R.P. (Eds) (2001, Summer) Theme: Engaging Anthropology in Disability Studies, Disability Studies Quarterly, 21 (3).

Lesnik-Oberstein, Karín (Eds) (2015) *Rethinking Disability Theory and Practice: Challenging Essentialism* (Houndmills: Palgrave Macmillan)

Linton, S. (1998) *Claiming Disability: Knowledge and Identity* (New York Univ. Press).

--------(2007) *My Body Politic: A Memoir* (Ann Arbor: Univ. of Michigan Press).

Longmore, P.K. (2003) *Why I Burned My Book and Other Essays on Disability* (Philadelphia: Temple University Press).

Marks, D. (1999) *Disability: Controversial Debates and Psychosocial Perspectives* (New York: Routledge).

Mitchell, D.T. and Snyder, S. L. (Eds)(1997) *The Body and Physical Difference: Discourses of disability* (Ann Arbor: University of Michigan Press).

Oliver, M. (1996) *Understanding Disability: From Theory to Practice* (Houndmills, Macmillan Pvt. Limited).

--------(1990) *The Politics of Disablement* (London: The MacMillan Press).

Prasher, V. P. (Ed) (2010) *Contemporary Issues in Intellectual Disabilities: Disability Studies* (New York: Nova Science Publishers, Inc.)

Ray, Sarah Jaquette and Sibara, Jay (Eds) (2017) *Disability Studies and the Environmental Humanities : Toward an Eco-Crip Theory* (University of Nebraska)

Reinders, H. (2000) *The Future of the Disabled in Liberal Society: An Ethical Analysis* (Notre Dame: University of Notre Dame Press).

Schillmeier, Michael (2010) *Rethinking Disability: Bodies, Senses, and Things* (New York: Routledge)

Shakespeare, T.(Ed)(1998) *The Disability Reader: Social Science Perspectives* (London/New York: Cassell).

Siebers, Tobin (2008) *Disability Theory—Corporealities: Discourses of Disability* (Ann Arbor: University of Michigan Press)

Snyder, S.L. et al (Eds) (2002) *Disability Studies: Enabling the Humanities* (New York: Modern Language Association Press).

Watson, Nick et al (2012) *Routledge Handbook of Disability Studies* (London and New York: Routledge)

MPDS 002: The Sociology of Disability and Rehabilitation

In this course, an attempt would be made to examine the sociological perspective to critically deconstruct traditional interpretations of the meaning of disability. Rather than accepting disability as an individual "problem" located within his or her body, mind or soul, it will focus on the cultural construction of ideas-such as, locomotor disability, mental retardation, autism, behavior disorders, and the myriad of other categories that often serve to cloak the humanness of millions of people worldwide.

Suggested Readings

Albrecht, G. L. (1992) *The Disability Business: Rehabilitation in America* (Newbury Park: Sage Publications).

--------et al (Eds) (2001) *Handbook of Disability Studies* (Thousand Oaks, California: Sage Publications).

Barnartt, S. and Scotch, R. (2001) *Disability Protests: Contentious Politics, 1970-1999* (Washington, DC: Gallaudet University Press).

Campbell, J. and Oliver, M. (1996) *Disability Politics: Understanding our Past, Changing our Future* (London and New York: Routledge).

Connor, David J. et al (Eds) (2014) *Practicing Disability Studies in Education: Acting Toward Social Change* (New York: Peter Lang Publishing)

Priestley, M. (1999) *Disability Politics and Community Care* (London: Jessica Kingsley Publlishers).

Skrtic, T. M. (Ed) (1995) *Disability and Democracy: Reconstructing Special Education for Postmodernity,* Special Education Series (New York: Teachers College Press).

Turner, David M. and Stagg, Kevin (Eds) (2006) *Social Histories of Disability and Deformity: Bodies, Images and Experiences* (London and New York: Routledge)

MPDS 003: Disability, Human Rights Law and Public Policy

Suggested Readings

Bartlett, P. et al (2007) *Mental Disability and the European Convention on Human Rights* (Leiden/Boston: Martinus Nijhoff Publishers).

Blanck, Peter (Ed) (2005) *Disability Rights* (Aldershot: Ashgate Publishing Limited).

Blanck, Peter and Flynn, Eilionóir (Eds) (2017) *Routledge Handbook of Disability Law and Human Rights* (New York and London: Routledge)

Charlton, J.I. (1998) *Nothing about us without us: Disability Oppression and Empowerment* (Berkeley: University of California Press).

Clare, E. (1999) *Exile & pride: Disability, queerness, and liberation* (Cambridge, MA: South End Press).

Clements, L. and Read, J. (Eds) (2008) *Disabled People and the Right to Life: The Protection and Violation Disabled People's Most Most Basic Human Rights* (Oxon: Routledge).

Degener, Theresia (2016) Disability in a Human Rights Context, *Laws*, 5 (35), pp. 1-24

Herr, S.S. et al (Eds) (2003) *The Human Rights of Persons with Intellectual Disabilities: Different but Equal* (Oxford/New York: Oxford Univ. Press).

Kanter, Arlene S. (2015) *The Development of Disability Rights under International Law: From Charity to Human Rights* (New York and London: Routledge)

Karna, G.N. (2008) Editorial: Disability rights in a global context, *International Journal of Therapy and Rehabilitation*, 15 (10), 01 Oct., pp 420-421.

--------(2002a) Disability and human rights: an international perspective, *International Journal of Disability Studies*, special issue on 'Disability and Human Rights', 1(1), Jan.-Mar., pp. 3-27.

--------(2002b) Disability and the politics of discrimination, *Human Rights Perspective*, 1 (1), pp.

--------(2000a) Impaired rehabilitation, *The Pioneer* (New Delhi), Jan. 24.

--------(2000b) Disabled human rights, *The Pioneer* (New Delhi), Feb.11.

--------(1999) *United Nations and the Rights of Disabled Persons: A Study in Indian Perspective* (New Delhi: APH Publishing Corporation).

--------and Gaharana, K. (1994) Disability and the rights of disabled persons, In: K.P. Saksena (Ed) *Human Rights: Perspective and Challenges beyond 1990s* (New Delhi: Lancer Books).

Krieger, L.H. (2003) *Backlash against the ADA: Reinterpreting Disability Rights* (Ann Arbor, MI: University of Michigan Press).

Nussbaum, M.C. (2006) *Frontiers of Justice: Disability, Nationality Species Membership* (Oxford University Press).

O' Brien, R. (Ed) (2004) *Voices from the Edge* (Oxford University Press).

Quinn, G. and Degener, T. (2002) *Human Rights and Disability* (New York: UN).

Raj, S.L. (1998) *Fifty Years after Freedom* (New Delhi: Indian Social Institute).

Rioux, Marcia H. et al (2011) *Critical Perspectives on Human Rights and Disability Law* (Leiden: Martinus Nijhoff Publishers)

Rispler - Chaim (2007) *Disability in Islamic Law* (The Netherlands: Springer).

Schlesinger, L. and Taub, D.E. (Eds)(2003) *Instructional Materials for Sociology and Disability Studies* (Washington, DC: ASA Teaching Resources Center).

Scotch, R. (2001) *From Good Will to Civil Rights: Transforming Federal Disability Policy* (Philadelphia: Temple University Press).

Shapiro, J.P. (1994) *No Pity* (New Delhi: Universal Law Publishing).

Silvers, A. et al (1998) *Disability Difference Discrimination: Perspectives on Justice in Bioethics and Public Policy* (Lanham: Rowman & Littlefield Publishers).

Stein, M.S. (2006) *Distributive Justice Disability Utilitarianism against Egalitarianism* (New Haven and London: Yale University Press).

Swain, J. et al (Eds) (1993) *Disabling Barriers Enabling Environments* (New Delhi: Sage Publications).

United Nations (2006) *United Nations Convention on Rights of Persons with Disabilities* (New York: United Nations).

--------(2007) From *Exclusion to Equality: Realizing the Rights of Persons with Disabilities*, Handbook for Parliamentarians on the Convention on the Rights of Persons with Disabilities and its Optional Protocol (Geneva).

Verma, S.K. (Ed) (2002) *Rights of Persons with Disabilities* (New Delhi: Indian Law Institute).

MPDS 004: Advanced Research Methodology and Statistical Techniques in Disability Studies

This course is intended to familiarize the scholars with the latest research methodologies as also tools and techniques developed in the field of Disability Studies. Among the topics identified for the course include Concepts in Interdisciplinary Research on Disability Studies, Quantitative Methods (containing inputs- such as, Formulation of sociological research questions and the logic of testing and inference; Major quantitative and qualitative methodologies with emphasis on former; Relationship between problems formulation, theoretical perspective, and research methods), Introduction to Qualitative Research (Developing and using qualitative methods used by sociologists to conduct research; Underlying assumptions and limitations), Participant Observation (Field techniques of participant observation, initiation of studies, the observer's role, use of indicators and working hypotheses, field notes; Social structure and process; Readings in representative studies using the method), Intermediate Social Statistics (Introduction to multivariate statistical techniques to social science data), Applications to issues of special education and related educational and human service settings.

Suggested Readings

Albrecht, G.L. et al (Eds) (2001) *Handbook of Disability Studies* (Thousand Oaks, California: Sage Publications).

--------(Eds) (2006) *Encyclopedia of Disability* (Thousand Oaks, California: Sage Publications).

Barnartt, Sharon (Ed) (2010) *Disability as a Fluid State* (Research in Social Science and Disability, Vol. 5 (Bingley: Emerald Group Publishing Limited)

Barnes, C. and Mercer, G. (Eds) (n.d.) *Doing Disability Research* (Leeds: The Disability Press).

--------(2003) *Disability* (Oxford: Polity Press). Barnes, C. et al (Eds) (2002) *Disability Studies Today* (Cambridge, UK: Polity).

Barton, L. and Oliver, M. (Eds) (1997) *Disability Studies: Past, Present and Future* (Leeds: The Disability Press).

Corker, M. and Shakespeare, T. (Eds) (2002) *Disability/ postmodernity: Embodying Disability Theory* (New York: Continuum).

Hagglund, Kristofer J. et al (Eds) (2006) *Handbook of Applied Disability and Rehabilitation Research* (New York: Springer Publishing Company)

Kroll, Thilo (Ed) (2007) *Focus on Disability: Trends in Research and Application*, Vol. II (New York: Nova Biomedical Books)

Marks, D. (1999) *Disability: Controversial Debates and Perspectives* (New York: Routledge).

Morris, Richard J. (Ed) (2005) *Disability Research and Policy: Current Perspectives* (Malwah New Jersey: Routledge)

Oliver, M. (1996) *Understanding Disability: From Theory to Practice* (New York: St. Martin's).

--------(1997) *The Politics of Disablement* (New York: St. Martin's).

Shakespeare, Tom (Ed) (2015) *Disability Research Today: International Perspectives* (London and New York: Routledge)

--------(Ed) (1988) *The Disability Reader: Social Science Perspectives* (London: Cassell).

Snyder, S. et al (Eds) (2002) *Disability Studies: Enabling the Humanities* (New York: Modern Language Association).

Van Manen, Max (1990) *Researching Lived Experience: Human Science for an Action Sensitive Pedagogy* (London Ontario: Althouse Press).

Wendell, S. (1996) *The Rejected Body: Feminist Philosophical Reflections on Disability* (New York: Routledge)

MPDS 005: Research Colloquium and Seminar on the chosen area for research work for MPhil programme (2 Credits)

An overview of critical approaches to dis/ability and inclusion. Analysis of shifting social and cultural constructions of dis/ability through an interdisciplinary exploration of autobiography, narrative, film, legal and policy issue and research literature.

MPDS 021: Disability Human Rights Law and Public Policy (3 Credits)

This is a unique blending of theoretical and applied research course. Apart from having rigorous examination of theoretical issues involved in promotion and protection of rights of persons with disabilities, the scholar will have to select a topic of interest to them and prepare a class or seminar presentation and paper on the topic. The topic may pertain to domestic, international, or comparative disability law and public policy. However, some grounding in Disability Studies or related field (e.g. rehabilitation science, education, social policy) is suggested.

Suggested Readings

Aggarwal, S. and Alkazi, R.M. (1991) *Exploring Care-taking Arrangement for Persons with Mental and Multiple Disabilities* (New Delhi: Alternative Strategies for the Handicapped).

Arneil, Barbara and Hirschman, Nancy J. (Eds) (2016) Disability and Political Theory (Cambridge: Cambridge University Press)

Baylies, C (2002) Disability and the notion of human development: questions of rights and capabilities, *Disability and Society*, 17(7), pp. 725-739.

Blanck, P. (Ed) (2005) *Disability Rights* (Aldershot: Ashgate Publishing Limited).

Herr, S.S. et al (Eds) (2003) *The Human Rights of Persons with Intellectual Disabilities: Different but Equal* (Oxford and New York: Oxford University Press).

Kanter, Arlene S. (2015) *The Development of Disability Rights under International Law: From Charity to Human Rights* (New York and London: Routledge)

Karna, G.N. (2008) Editorial: Disability rights in a global context, *International Journal of Therapy and Rehabilitation*, 15 (10), 01 Oct., pp.420-421.

--------(2002a) Disability and human rights: an international perspective, *International Journal of Disability Studies*, special issue on 'Disability and Human Rights', 1(1), Jan.-Mar., pp. 3-27.

--------(2002b) Disability and the politics of discrimination, *Human Rights Perspective*, 1 (1), pp.

--------(2001) *Disability Studies in India: Retrospects and Prospects* (New Delhi: Gyan Publishing House).

--------(2000a) Impaired rehabilitation,*The Pioneer* (New Delhi), Jan. 24.

--------(2000b) Disabled human rights, *The Pioneer* (New Delhi), Feb.11.

--------(1999) *United Nations and the Rights of Disabled Persons: A Study in Indian Perspective* (New Delhi: APH Publishing Corporation).

--------and Gaharana, K. (1994) Disability and the rights of disabled persons, In: K.P. Saksena (Ed) *Human Rights: Perspective and Challenges beyond 1990s* (New Delhi: Lancer Books).

Nussbaum, M.C. (2006) *Frontiers of Justice: Disability, Nationality Species Membership* (Oxford University Press).

O' Brien, R. (Ed) (2004) *Voices from the Edge* (Oxford University Press). Rispler-Chaim (2007) *Disability in Islamic Law* (The Netherlands: Springer).

United Nations (2006) *United Nations Convention on Rights of Persons with Disabilities* (New York: United Nations).

--------(2007) From *Exclusion to Equality: Realizing the Rights of Persons with Disabilities,* Handbook for Parliamentarians on the Convention on the Rights of Persons with Disabilities and its Optional Protocol (Geneva).

2nd Semester

MPDS 022: Representation of Ability/Disability (3 Credits)

Ability and disability are the key concepts in education. This course provides an opportunity to examine how ability and disability are presented in popular culture, literature as well as film, autobiographies of people with and without disabilities, and in professional texts/narratives (e.g., research literature, practitioner materials) and the meaning of this representations for educational practice and social policy. Besides considering different constructions and meanings of ability and disability, participants will get the chance to examine markers of privilege as well as processes of marginalization. Thus, this course is completely focussed on developing skills to examine how ideas (including ideas about the body and mind) are constructed and represented in cultural and social contexts.

Suggested Readings

Albrecht, G.L. et al (Eds) (2001) *Handbook of Disability Studies* (Thousand Oaks, CA: Sage).

Barnes, C. (1992) *Disabling Imagery and the Media* (Halifax: Ryburn and British Council of Disabled People–BCODP).

Crutchfield, S. and Epstein, M. (Eds) (2000) *Points of Contact: Disability, Art, and Culture* (Ann Arbor: University of Michigan Press).

Davis, L. (1995) *Enforcing Normalcy: Disability, Deafness, and the Body* (New York: Verso).

Deutsch, H. and Nussbaum, F. (Eds) (2000) *DEFECT! Engendering the Modern Body* (Ann Arbor: University of Michigan Press).

Fraser, Benjamin (Ed) (2016) *Cultures of Representation: Disability in World Cinema Contexts* (London: Wallflower Press)

Gartner, A. and Joe, T. (Eds) (1987) *Images of the Disabled, Disabling Images* (New York: Praeger).

Gerber, D. (2000) *Disabled Veterans in History* (Ann Arbor: Univ. of Michigan Press).

Hall, Alice (2016) *Literature and Disability* (London and New York: Routledge)

Holmes, M.S. (2004) *Fictions of Affliction* (Ann Arbor: Univ. of Michigan Press).

Karna, G.N. (2001) *Disability Studies in India: Retrospects and Prospects* (New Delhi: Gyan Publishing House).

--------(1999) *United Nations and Rights of Disabled Persons: A Study in Indian Perspective* (New Delhi: APH).

Linett, Maren Tova (2017) *Bodies of Modernism: Physical Disability in Transatlantic Modernist Literature* (Ann Arbor: University of Michigan Press)

Meekosha, H. (2005) *Body Battles: Disability, Representation,and Participation* (Thousand Oaks, CA: Sage).

Mitchell, D. and Snyder, S. (Eds) (1997) *The Body and Physical Difference: Discourses of Disability* (Ann Arbor: University of Michigan Press).

--------(2000) *Narrative Prosthesis: Disability and the Dependencies of Discourse* (Ann Arbor: University of Michigan Press).

Mossman, Mark (2009) *Disability, Representation and the Body in Irish Writing: 1800-1922* (Houndmills: Palgrave Macmillan)

Shakespeare, T. (1994) Cultural representation of disabled people: dustbins for disavowal?, *Disability & Society,* 9, pp. 283-299.

Stainton, T. (2003) Reason's other: the emergence of the disabled subject in the Northern Renaissance, *Disability & Society,* 9, pp. 225-243.

Thiher, A. (2000) *Revels in Madness: Insanity in Medicine and Literature* (Ann Arbor: University of Michigan Press).

Thomson, R.G. (1996) *Extraordinary Bodies* (New York: Columbia University Press).

--------(1996) *Freakery: Cultural Spectacles of the Extraordinary Body* (New York: New York University Press).

Ville, I. et al (1994) Self-representations and physical impairment: a social constructionist approach, *Sociology of Health & Illness,* 16, pp. 301-321.

MPDS 023: Seminar on Disability Studies (1 Credit)

Seminar Presentation is a core component of the syllabus on Disability Studies. Through readings and discussions, participants examine disability as a social and cultural construct and political-legal and rights- based issue. The seminar is organized as a discussion group, and participants are expected to assume responsibility for organizing discussions. Suggested Readings for the seminar would include both "classics" and recently published works on contemporary themes in Disability Studies.

MPDS 024: Fieldwork in Disability Services (2 Credits)

This course provides the scholar an opportunity to gain experiential learning regarding the lived experiences of the persons with disabilities in terms of their family and social life as also status as citizens of the country. Students are assigned to work under the supervision of a mentor from the faculty and also outside mentor to whom they are to be attached for completing the assignment.

MPDS 025: Internship in Disability Studies (Non-Credit)

Under the internship, the scholar will have to make the first hand experience about the functioning of reputed academic institutions/organizations and advocacy groups working for offering courses (in DS)/delivery of services/ ensuring justice/empowering the persons with disabilities. If the scholar wishes, he/she could get affiliated to and stay at universities/institutions abroad where degrees/diplomas on Disability Studies are imparted.

3rd and 4th Semester

MPDS 026: Dissertation

Dissertation comprises of two parts: one 5,000 word essay outlining the research topic, and a 15,000-17,000 word dissertation. The topic of the dissertation has to be selected by the scholar in consultation of the mentor/supervisor. For preparing a balanced, theoretically sound and scientifically arranged synopsis/research proposal, an in- depth study of the published literature is highly required. The additional length of the dissertation would help the scholar to utilise knowledge and skills gained from previous courses and to explore and research your chosen topic in more detail. The dissertation may be a secondary analysis or an empirical study of a previously unstudied topic.

PhD in Disability Studies

PhD in Disability Studies (PhDDS)

The PhD programme in Disability Studies is intended for those students who wish to further develop their critical understanding of disability both as an independent issue and as an issue that raises fundamental questions relating to the meaning of equality, legal distinctions of classes of people, issues of difference as a social category, applied human rights, the social and legal construction of inequality, and the implications of inclusion as opposed to add-on programs and services.

All PhD candidates are required to develop a plan of study providing an integrated, coherent rationale for their studies as they relate to coursework, the comprehensive examination and the dissertation. The plan of study must demonstrate the use of critical theory in Disability Studies as well as an interdisciplinary approach that charts new areas in scholarship in this field. Upon admission, each student is assigned a mentor/supervisor, based on student's field of interest as indicated in statement of interest and advisor's area of expertise, with whom the student meets to decide on the plan of study. The plan must be approved by both the student's supervisor and the Centre Director or Department Head during the first term of study. By the end of the second term, the student must submit a finalized plan of study, which is a refinement of the first. Upon completion of their first year of study, students are required to choose a supervisor.

Duration

Normally, the duration of PhD in Disability Studies (PhDDS) will be minimum three years, to be extendable on merit by further two years in extraordinary situations.

Admission Requirements

The PhD in Disability Studies (PhDDS) is open to qualified and highly motivated students with abiding interest to obtain advanced scholarly knowledge and training in the interdisciplinary area of Disability Studies and those who have demonstrated academic excellence in allied areas. To be eligible for admission, candidates must:

- have completed a master's degree with a minimum (A-) average or equivalent; equivalence is demonstrated by five or more years of voluntary or paid work experience in a senior position in government, administrative position in an NGO, teaching or administrative position in a university, college or high school, within the area of social justice, human rights and disability;

- provide a statement of interest demonstrating commitment to advanced work in Disability Studies. The statement should include a discussion of the applicant's background, interests, skills and career goals, along with a proposed program of study and specific research interests;
- demonstrate ability in writing and research by submitting a recent research paper or report that the applicant has written for a course or in an employment context; and
- provide two letters of reference, preferably one from the Centre/University faculty members. Equivalencies (letters from non-university faculty) are considered for applicants who have been out of school for more than five years.

Programme Components

The PhD in Disability Studies will have two major components: coursework and dissertation, accounting for 32 Credits (including 4 Credits each for three courses and 20 Credits for Thesis).

PhDDS 027: Doctoral Seminar in Disability Studies (4 Credits)

PhDDS 028: Research Seminar with a Required Major Paper (4 Credits)

PhDDS 029: Major Research Paper (4 Credits)

PhDDS 030: Thesis (20 Credits)

1st Year (Two Semesters)

Courses

PhDDS 027: Doctoral Seminar in Disability Studies (4 Credits)

This course provides a broad overview of key texts in the field of Disability Studies, as well as an in-depth analysis of competing and complementary views about how 'disability' is defined. Areas to be studied include social movement theory and how this theory is reflected in the context of disability activism; tension and collaboration between academics and grass roots activists; gaps in Disability Studies; marginalization between and among people with disabilities; the notion of a disability community or communities; disability and the law; race, class, gender, and poverty; disability culture and literature; and social policy and the political economy of disability. The seminar also covers disability issues in the developing world and in Europe, including a comparative study of national and international laws pertaining to disability rights protection and the connections between disability rights and human rights, locally, regionally and internationally.

Suggested Readings

Albrecht, G.L. et al (Eds) (2001) *Handbook of Disability Studies* (Thousand Oaks, California: Sage Publications).

--------(Eds)(2006) *Encyclopedia of Disability* (Thousand Oaks, California: Sage Publications).

Barnes, C. and Mercer, G. (2003) *Disability* (Oxford: Polity Press).

--------et al (Eds) (1999) *Exploring Disability: A Sociological Introduction* (Cambridge: Polity Press).

Barton, L. and Oliver, M. (Eds) (1997) *Disability Studies: Past, Present and Future* (Leeds: The Disability Press).

Butler, R. and Parr, H. (Eds) (2005) *Mind and Body Space: Geographies of Illness, Impairment and Disability* (London and New York: Routledge).

Danforth, S. and Gabel, S.L. (Eds) (2006) *Vital Questions facing Disability Studies in Education* (New York: Peter Lang).

Davis, L.J. (Ed.)(1997) *The Disability Studies Reader* (New York: Routledge).

Dell Orto, A.E. and Marinelli, R.P. (Eds) (1995) *Encyclopedia of Disability and Rehabilitation* (Macmillan Library Reference USA).

Gabel, S. (Ed) (2005) *Disability Studies in Education: Readings in Theory and Method* (New York: Peter Lang).

Johnstone, D. (1998) *An Introduction to Disability Studies* (London: David Fulton Publishers).

Kanter, Arlene S. (2015) *The Development of Disability Rights under International Law* (New York and London: Routledge)

Karna, G.N. (2007) Disability studies in India: new directions for future, Disability Studies in Higher Education: *Monograph Series No. 2* (New Delhi: Society for Disability and Rehabilitation Studies).

--------(2001) *Disability Studies in India: Retrospects and Prospects* (New Delhi: Gyan Publishing House).

--------(1999a) *United Nations and Rights of Disabled Persons: A Study in Indian Perspective* (New Delhi: APH Publishing Corporation).

--------(1999b) Disabled perspective, *The Pioneer* (New Delhi), Dec. 8.

Kristiansen, K. (2008) *Arguing about Disability: Philosophical Perspectives* (London: Routledge).

Linton, S. (1998) *Claiming Disability: Knowledge and Identity* (New York: New York University Press).

Longmore, P.K. (2003) *Why I Burned My Book and Other Essays on Disability* (Philadelphia: Temple University Press).

Mitchell, D. and Snyder, S. (Eds) (1997) *The Body and Physical Difference: Discourses of Disability* (Ann Arbor: University of Michigan Press).

Nussbaum, M.C. (2006) *Frontiers of Justice: Disability, Nationality Species Membership* (Oxford University Press).

Oliver, M. (1996) *Understanding Disability: From Theory to Practice* (Houndmills: Macmillan Pvt. Limited).

--------and N. Watson (2001) The social model of disability: an outdated ideology?, *Research in Social Science and Disability,* 2, pp 9-28.

Perkins, M. (2007) *Pragmatic Impairment* (Cambridge University Press).

Quinn, P. (1998) *Understanding Disability: A Lifespan Approach* (Thousand Oaks: California; Sage Publications).

Shakespeare, Tom (Ed) (2015) *Disability Research Today: International Perspectives* (London and New York: Routledge)

Sheila, A.M.M. and Williamson, L. (2007) *Impairment and Disability: Law and Ethics at the Beginning and End of Life* (New York: Routledge-Cavendish).

PhDDS 028: Research Seminar with a Required Major Paper (4 Credits)

This required seminar enables students to engage in either secondary analysis or original research on a topic related to the human rights approach to disability. Emphasis will be placed on the development and demonstration of skills including: question formulation, problem solving, data collection and analysis, proof and communication. This seminar provides the guidance for the major research paper that students must complete as a programme requirement.

PhDDS 029: Major Research Paper (4 Credits)

The research paper tests students from the standpoint of educational objectives of breadth, depth, synthesis and originality; trains students in the recognition, formulation and writing up of a specific project; and gives students experience of working independently on a project under faculty supervision. Students are supervised on a small group basis and exceptions are made for students who have interests in specific areas to be supervised by faculty members with related expertise.

The students are required to complete the aforesaid three courses during two semesters of the first year and after satisfactory completion of these three papers with the minimum score of grade 'A minus' (7 points), he/she will have to select the topic for doctoral research work in consultation with the identified mentor/supervisor after in-depth study on any particular area of Disability Studies from interdisciplinary perspective, as much as possible. The student will have to prepare a Synopsis of PhD research work accordingly after extensive study of the literature. The doctoral candidate will be called to face the viva – voce at two levels—firstly before the Centre or Department faculty and then, the Board of Studies of the concerned School/Faculty of the University. As per the rules and regulations of the concerned University and also guidelines of the UGC, the proposal will be placed for consideration for approval before the Board of Studies on the basis of recommendation made by the Centre or Department faculty. The student will get formally registered for PhD degree when the PhD Synopsis is approved by the Board of Studies of the concerned University.

The doctoral Thesis will be evaluated by two outside examiners (who are leading experts on the topic/theme) and the Viva- Voce could be held by the University only after getting their positive recommendations and good comments. If the outside experts give favourable and positive comments, the doctoral candidate will be called to defend his/her doctoral Thesis at the Viva-Voce. The PhD degree could be conferred only after getting a recommendation to this effect by the outside examiners, based on Thesis as also performance at the Viva-Voce.

PG Diploma in Disability Studies (with Concentration on Innovations in Rehabilitation Technology)

About the Programme

PG Diploma in Disability Studies—PGDRT (with Concentration on Innovations in Rehabilitation Technology) is intended to impart theoretical knowledge and training to the professionals wishing to have sound understanding about delivery of state-of-the-art Indianised version of assistive technology devices to the persons with physical, cognitive and/or sensory disabilities. The PGDRT would be a unique programme of its kind to be offered in Rehabilitation Technology with Disability Studies components. The programme's interdisciplinary orientation is informed by various academic fields—such as, architecture, bio- medical science, civil engineering, rehabilitation science, anthropology, geography, bio- technology, management, economics, education, political science, social work, sociology, women's/ gender studies, human rights, refugee and immigration studies, history and aging studies. Theories of human rights form the basis for understanding how existing legal, economic and social rationales for inclusion relate to systemic inequality and oppression.

Offered on a full time (one and a half year- three semesters) basis, the PG Diploma in Disability Studies (with Concentration on Innovations in Rehabilitation Technology) provides an innovative area of study and research for inter-disciplinary professionals with varied backgrounds interested in working in disability sector, including rehabilitation technologists, architecturists, educationists, management personnel, policy makers and disability rights activists. This programme is basically designed for all professionals serving individuals with assistive technology needs in the areas of occupational therapy, physical therapy, speech language pathology, special education, engineering, or vocational counselors/instructors.

The Objectives of PG Diploma in Disability Studies (with Concentration on Innovations in Rehabilitation Technology) are as hereunder:

- To familiarize the students with the basic theoretical underpinnings and contours of Rehabilitation Technology for empowering the persons with disabilities;
- To understand the basic application of research principles to rehabilitation, such as the evaluation of personal practice, utilization of consumer satisfaction surveys, conducting needs analysis, etc;
- To use problem-solving skills to assist the persons with disabilities in attaining individualized goals suited to their abilities and needs;
- To utilize rehabilitation technology and adapted computer applications in service delivery;

- To provide consumers with information and assistance about human, legal, and civil rights so that they will be empowered to speak on their own behalf and obtain assistance when necessary;
- To identify the primary rehabilitation techniques employed to evaluate, train, and identify employment and independent living options for persons with disabilities;
- To present theories of human rights as a basis for understanding existing legal, economic and social rationales for inclusion in relation to systemic barriers and oppression;
- To situate key debates in Disability Studies in both historical and contemporary contexts—including understanding how issues relating to disability are interpreted and advanced in both an academic setting and in public as also private policy/programming;
- To apply qualitative and quantitative research skills to policy research and longitudinal studies; and
- To provide a national platform for career in advanced study and research in the field of Disability Studies with focus on latest innovations in Rehabilitation Technology.

Eligibility for Admission

Bachelor's degree in any stream of knowledge including rehabilitation science, social science, management, education, natural sciences, engineering, life sciences or allied areas, under 10+2+3 pattern of education with the minimum score of 60% marks.

Course Requirements

The duration of PG Diploma in Disability Studies (with Concentration on Innovations in Rehabilitation Technology) is 18 months. Students opting for this diploma programme will have to take ten core and two elective courses (excluding Dissertation and Internship) in fulfillment for requirements for the award of diploma.

*Minimum credit requirements = 58 (Duration : 3 semesters: CGPA requirements 7.0)

The first year (comprising two semesters of 6 months' duration each) of the programme would have 32 Credits to be divided into ten Compulsory and any two (out of three) Elective Courses. Each course has 4 Credits, except the dissertation (8 Credits) and internship (2 Credits). The 3rd semester is exclusively for writing a Dissertation under the direction of mentor/supervisor. The course titles as also required credits are given semester- wise:

- PGDRT 001: Basic Concepts and Theories of Disability Studies (Core paper) 4 Credits
- PGDRT 002: Introduction to Assistive Technology Services (Core paper) 4 Credits
- PGDRT 003: Architecture Designing and Management (Core paper) 4 Credits
- PGDRT 004: Disability in the Age of ICT (Core paper) 4 Credits
- PGDRT 005: Computers, Communication and Control Systems (Core paper) 4 Credits
- PGDRT 006: Adaptive Equipment Design and Fabrication (Core paper) 4 Credits
- PGDRT 007: Assistive Technology for Literacy, Learning, and Participation in Pre-Primary to Higher Education (Core paper) 4 Credits
- PGDRT 008: Seating and Wheelchair Mobility (Core paper) 4 Credits
- PGDRT 009: Augmentative Communication Assessment & Development (Elective paper) 4 Credits)
- PGDRT 010: History and Theory in the Built Environment (Elective paper) 4 Credits
- PGDRT 011: Facilities Management : Theory and Practice (Elective paper) 4 Credits
- PGDRT 012: Fieldwork/Experimentation in Disability Rehabilitation Services (Core paper) 4 Credits
- PGDRT 013: Built Environment and Cost-Benefit Analysis (Core paper) 4 Credits

- PGDRT 014: Internship in Rehabilitation Technology- full time (2 Credits)
- PGDRT 015: Dissertation (8 Credits)

1st Semester

PGDRT 001: Basic Concepts and Theories of Disability Studies

This course provides a broad overview of definitions and paradigms of impairment and disability: medical, psychological, socio-political and marxist theoretical perspectives; functionalist, role theory, interactionism, disability and human rights issue, and recent developments in feminist and postmodern approaches to disability. This course draws on various disciplinary perspectives to understand the broad and complex phenomenon of disability in historical perspective, as represented in literature and culture, and as it impinges on issues of broad public concern today. Attention is given to the implications of theory and practice for the lives of persons with disabilities.

Suggested Readings

Albrecht, G. L. et al (Eds) (2001) *Handbook of Disability Studies* (Thousand Oaks, CA: Sage Publications).

--------(Eds) (2006) *Encyclopedia of Disability* (Thousand Oaks, CA: Sage Publications).

Barnes, C. and Mercer, G. (Eds) (2002) *Disability Studies Today* (Cambridge: Polity Press).

--------et al (Eds) (1999) *Exploring Disability: A Sociological Introduction* (Cambridge: Polity Press).

Barton, L. and Oliver, M. (Eds) (1997) *Disability Studies: Past, Present and Future* (Leeds: The Disability Press).

Davis, L.J. (Ed.) (1997) *The Disability Studies Reader* (New York: Routledge).

Davis, L. and Linton, S. (1995) Disability Studies [Feature issue], *Radical Teacher*, fall, No. 47.

Johnstone, D. (1998) *An Introduction to Disability Studies* (London: David Fulton Publishers).

Karna, G.N. (2008) Disability studies in India: new directions for future, Disability Studies in Higher Education: Monograph Series No. 2 (New Delhi: Society for Disability and Rehabilitation Studies).

--------(2007) Promotion of Disability Studies in Education, *Monograph Series No. 1 : Disability Studies in India: Role of Institutions of Higher Education* (New Delhi: Society for Disability and Rehabilitation Studies).

--------(2001) *Disability Studies in India: Retrospects and Prospects* (New Delhi: Gyan Publishing House).

--------(2000c) Disability Studies in India: issues and challenges, *International Journal of Disability Studies*, inaugural issue on 'Disability and Social Policy in the New Millennium',1(1),Oct.-Dec., pp. 20-40.

Linton, S. (1998) *Claiming Disability: Knowledge and Identity* (New York Univ. Press).

Longmore, P.K. (2003) *Why I Burned My Book and Other Essays on Disability* (Philadelphia: Temple University Press).

Oliver, M. (1996) *Understanding Disability: From Theory to Practice* (Houndmills: Macmillan Pvt. Limited).

WHO (1980) *International Classification of Impairments, Disabilities, and Handicaps: A Manual of Classification Relating to the Consequences of Disease* (Geneva).

--------(2001) *International Classification of Functioning, Disability, and Health* (Geneva).

PGDRT 002: Introduction to Assistive Technology Services

This course examines the best clinical practices and state-of-the-art Assistive Technology devices, including the areas of Augmentative Communication, Cognitive Technologies, Computer Access, Environmental Control, Home Modification, Orthotics and Prosthetics, Seating and Wheeled Mobility, and Worksite Modification. Funding and Outcomes Measurement with respect to each area also included.

Suggested Readings

Adlam, T. et al (2004) The installation and support of internationally distributed equipment for people with dementia, *IEEE transactions on information technology in biomedicine*, 8 (3), pp. 253-257.

Bates, R. and Jones, M. (2003) Using Computer Software To Develop Switch Skills *[Technology and Persons with Disabilities] Conference Proceedings*. http://www.csun.edu/cod/conf/2003/proceedings/6.htm. Retrieved 2007-02-08.

Behrmann, M. and Schaff, J. (2001) Assisting educators with assistive technology: Enabling children to achieve independence in living and learning, *Children and Families* 42(3), pp. 24-28.

Bishop, J. (2003) The Internet for educating individuals with social impairments, *Journal of Computer Assisted Learning*, 19(4), 546-556.

Cain, S. (2001) *Accessing Technology - Using technology to support the learning and employment opportunities for visually impaired users* (Royal National Institute for the Blind).

Cincotti, F. (2008) Research report: Non-invasive brain-computer interface system: Towards its application as assistive technology, *Brain Research Bulletin*, 75, pp. 796-803

Cook, A. and Hussey, S. (2002) *Assistive Technologies- Principles and Practice*, 2nd Edition (Mosby).

Edwards, A.D.N., (Ed.) (1995) *Extra-Ordinary Human-Computer Interaction: Interfaces for Users with Disabilities*. Cambridge Series on Human-Computer Interaction. New York, Cambridge University Press. (Also available as part of the CD-rom, Overcoming Barriers: Theory and Practice in Disability, Cambridge University Press, 1999).

Franklin, K.S. (1991) Supported employment and assistive technology-A powerful partnership, In: S. L. Griffin & W.G. Revell (Eds) *Rehabilitation counselor desktop guide to supported employment* (Richmond, VA: Virginia Commonwealth University Rehabilitation Research and Training Center on Supported Employment).

Galvin, J.C. and McLaurin, C.A. (1991) A History of Rehabilitation Engineering, *REHAB Management*, August/September, pp. 70-77.

Gitlin, L. (1995) Why Older People Accept or Reject Assistive Technology, *Generations* (Spring), pp. 41-46.

Hammel, J. (2006) Aids for Activities of Daily Living, In: Gary L. Albrecht et al (Eds) *Enclyclopedia of Disability,* vol. 1 (Thousand Oaks: Sage Publications).

--------et al (2002) The Impact of Assistive Technology and Environmental Interventions on Function and Living Situation Status for People Who Are Aging with Developmental Disabilities, *Disability and Rehabilitation,* 24(1-3), pp. 93-105.

Hawes, P. and Blenkhorn, P. (2002) Bridging the Gap between Aspiration and Capability for Aphasic and Brain Injured People *[Technology and Persons with Disabilities]Conference Proceedings;* available at: http://www.csun.edu/cod/conf/2002/proceedings/220.htm

Hoenig, H. et al (2003) Does Assistive Technology Substitute for Personal Assistance among the Disabled Elderly?, *American Journal of Public Health,* 93(2), pp. 330-337.

Lahm, E. and Morrissette, S. (1994, April) Zap 'em with assistive technology, Paper presented at the annual meeting of The Council for Exceptional Children, Denver, CO.

LaPlante, M.P. et al (1997) The Prevalence of Need for Assistive Technology Devices and Home Accessibility Features, *Technology & Disability,* 6(1/2), pp. 17-28.

Lee, C. (1999) *Learning disabilities and assistive technologies; an emerging way to touch the future* (Amherst, MA: McGowan Publications).

Mann, W.C. et al (1999) Effectiveness of Assistive Technology and Environmental Interventions in Maintaining Independence and Reducing Home Care Costs for the Frail Elderly: A Randomized Controlled Trial, *Archives of Family Medicine,* 8, pp. 210-217.

McKeown, S. (2000) *Unlocking Potential - How ICT can support children with special needs* (The Questions Publishing Company Ltd.).

Nisbet, P. and Poon, P. (1998) *Special Access Technology* (The CALL Centre: University of Edinburgh).

Nisbet, P. et al (1999) *Supportive Writing Technology* (The CALL Centre: University of Edinburgh).

Orpwood, R. (1990) Design methodology for aids for the disabled, *Journal of Medical Engineering Technology*, Jan-Feb., 14(1), pp. 2-10.

Pain, H. et al (2003) *Choosing Assistive Devices: A Guide for Users and Professionals* (London: Jessica Kingsley Publishers).

Poulson, D. et al (Eds) (1996) *Userfit. A Practical Handbook on User-centred Design for Assistive Technology* (TIDE USER consortium).

Philips, B. and Zhao, H. (1993) Predictors of Assistive Technology Abandonment, *Assistive Technology*, 5, pp. 36-45.

Rothstein, L. (1991) Campuses and the Disabled, *The Chronicle of Higher Education*, September 4, pp. B4, B10.

Scherer, M.J. (2005) *Living in the State of Stuck: How Assistive Technology Impacts the Lives of People with Disabilities*, 4th edn.(Cambridge, MA: Brookline Books).

--------(2004) *Connecting to Learn: Educational and Assistive Technology for People with Disabilities* (Washington, DC: American Psychological Association Books).

--------(Ed) (2002) *Assistive Technology: Matching Device and Consumer for Successful Rehabilitation* (Washington, DC: APA Books).

Swann, J.I. (2007) *Promoting independence and activity in older people* (Quay Books).

Van der Heijden, D. (2007) How Does Alternative Access to Computers Work?, June 26, 2007.

Verbrugge, L. and Sevak, P. (2002) Use, Type, and Efficacy of Assistance for Disability, *Journal of Gerontology Social Sciences*, 57B(6), pp. S366-S379.

PGDRT 003: Architecture Designing and Management

This course deals with the project management context within which architecture is practiced. Students will study the development of professional expertise, and be introduced to the methods used to generate work and charge fees. The course will also address the project briefing and contract administration phases of an architectural project, including the development of a design brief and project feasibility analysis, development and contract law, project management frameworks, consultancy agreements, and the administration of a standard form lump sum building contract.

Suggested Readings

Abend, A.C. et al (1979) *Facilities for Special Education Services: A Guide for Planning New and Renovated Schools* (Baltimore: Maryland State Department of Education).

Ansley, J. (2000) Creating Accessible Schools (Washington, D.C.: National Clearinghouse for Educational Facilities); available at: http://www.edfacilities.org

Babbitt, B. et al (2002) The movement of accessible design principles into mainstream engineering: Now and then, *In: J.M. Winters et al (Eds) Emerging and Accessible Telecommunications, Information and Healthcare Technologies (RESNA Press), pp. 2-18).*

Boissevain, G. W.O. and Prins, M. (1995) Architectural management and design management - the state of the art in Netherlands and ideas for research, *International Journal of Architectural Management, Practice and Research*, 9.

Bourke, A. et al (1998) Universal instruction design in higher education: An approach for inclusion, *Equity & Excellence in Education, 31*(2), pp. 47-51.

Clarke, K. et al (2003) Designing acceptable 'smart' home technology to support people in the home, *Technology and Disability, 15*(3), pp. 191-199.

Cross, M. (1999) Accessing the Inaccessible: Disability and Archaeology, *Archaeological Review from Cambridge*, 15(2), pp. 7-30.

Danford, G.S. and Tauke, B. (Eds) (2002) *Universal Design (New York).*

Davenport, R. et al (2003) Assistive environments for successful aging, *In: M. Mokhtari (Ed) Independent living for persons with disabilities and elderly people, 1st International Conference on Smart Homes and Health Telematics, Assistive Technology Research Series (IOS Press), 12,* pp. 104-110.

Deyer, J.W. (2005) Decoding accessible-design terms, *PN/ Paraplegia News, 59*(1), pp. 24-28.

Drill, H. (2005) A closer look: A move toward accessible hotels, *PN/Paraplegia News, 59*(1), pp. 53-55.

Emmitt, S. (2001) Architectural management—an evolving field, *Engineering Construction and Architectural Management,* 6 (2).

--------(2007) *Design Management for Architects* (Oxford: Blackwell Publishing).

--------et al (2009) *Architectural Management: International Research and Practice* (Oxford: Wiley-Blackwell).

Government of India (undated) *Planning a Barrier Free Environment* (New Delhi: Office of the Chief Commissioner for Persons with Disabilities).

Higgins, C. (2002) Physically accessible housing, *Research Information on Independent Living, 1*(9).

Kose, S. (1998) From barrier-free to universal design: An international perspective, *Assistive Technology, 10*(1), pp. 44-50.

Mace, R.L. (1998) Universal design in housing, *Assistive Technology,10*(1), pp. 21-28.

Maisel, J.L. (2006) Toward inclusive housing and neighborhood design: a look at visitability, *Community Development: Journal of the Community Development Society, 37*(3), pp. 26-34.

Menendez, F. (2006) Access through architecture: Accessible classroom, *PN/Paraplegia News, 60* (10), pp. 20-26.

Nicolle, C. and Abascal, J. (Eds) *Inclusive Design Guidelines for HCI* (London and New York: Taylor & Francis).

Pace, R.J. and Young, L. (2002) Future housing now: The next generation universal home, In: *R. Simpson (Ed) Proceedings of the RESNA 25th International Conference: Technology and Disability: Research, Design, Practice and Policy* (Arlington, VA: RESNA Press).

Panek, P. et al (2001) Smart Home Applications for disabled Persons - Experiences and Perspectives; Reprint from "EIB Event 2001 - Proceedings"; (2001), S. 71-80; available at: http://publik.tuwien.ac.at/files/pub-et_4384.pdf

Peterson, W. (1998) Public policy affecting universal design, *Assistive Technology, 10*(1), 13-20.

Pullin, Graham (2009) *Design Meets Disability* (Cambridge: MIT Press)

PGDRT 004: Disability in the Age of Information Technology

This course is intended to examine the concepts and experience of disability in relation to recent innovations in information technology and communicative innovation. However, the focus would be on relationships between technological innovation and societal definition of disability; the dissemination of information; the potential of new technology for empowerment/disablement, and ethical issues of technological research. ICTs - combined with proper methodologies - can offer individuals the ability to compensate for physical or functional limitations, thus allowing them to enhance their social and economic integration in communities by enlarging the scope of activities available to them. By collaborating with other institutions that share these concerns the UNESCO is seeking to realize the full potential of ICTs and promote education and information for all within its mandate.

Suggested Readings

Aparna, M. (2008) ICT for Disability, M. Tech. Dissertation (Mumbai: Department of Computer Science and Engineering, Indian Institute of Technology, Bombay).

Aspinall, A. and Hegarty, J.R. (2001) ICT for adults with learning disabilities: An organisationwide audit, *British Journal of Educational Technology, 32*(3), pp. 365-372.

Bennett, J. et al (2002) *Rehabilitation Engineering Research Center on Recreational Technologies and Exercise Physiology Benefiting Persons with Disabilities (REC-TEC).*

Blischak, D.M. and Schlosser, R. W. (2003) Use of technology to support independent spelling by students with autism, *Topics in Language Disorders, 23*(4), pp. 293-304.

Braddock, D. (2004) Emerging Technologies and Cognitive Disability, *Journal of Special Education Technology,* 19(4), fall; available at: http://www.colemaninstitute.org/article_braddock_1.pdf

Bruyère, S.M. et al (2006) Information technology (IT) accessibility: Implications for employment of people with disabilities, *Work: A Journal of Prevention, Assessment and Rehabilitation*, 27 (4).

Dario, P. et al (1999) MOVAID: A personal robot in everyday life of disabled and elderly people, *Technology and Disability, 10*(2), pp. 77-93.

Davies, D. K. et al (2003) Utilization of Computer Technology to Facilitate Money Management by Individuals with Mental Retardation, *Education and Training in Mental Retardation and Developmental Disabilities, 38*(1), pp. 106-112.

Digital Angel (2002) *The Digital Angel Personal Safety and Location System with GPS Technology,* retrieved from: http://www.digitalangel.net/default.asp.

Douglas, G. (2002) ICT, Education, and Visual Impairment, British Journal of Educational Technology, 32 (3), pp. 353-364.

Lazar, Jonathan and Stein, Michael Ashley (Eds) (2017) *Disability, Human Rights, and Information Technology* (Philadelphia: University of Pennsylvania Press)

Mackelprang, R.W. and Salsgiver, R. O. (1998) *Disability: A Diversity Model Approach in Human Service Practice* (Washington, Lyceum).

Potter, J. and Wetherell, M. (1987) *Discourse and Social Psychology* (London: Sage).

Shakespeare, T. (1996) Disability, Identity and Difference, In: Colin Barnes and Geof Mercer (Eds) *Exploring the Divide* (Leeds: The Disability Press), pp. 94-113.

Technology for Disabled People (undated) available at: http://www.livingwithcerebralpalsy.com/ technologyinformation. php

The Access Technology Handbook Giving visually impaired users access to your Disability Unit or ICT Laboratory (Sensory Solutions (Pty) Ltd, 2008); available at: http://www.sensorysolutions.co.za/PDF/GeneralInfo/ The%20Disability%20Handbook%20-%20Volume%201%20-%20The%20ICT%20laboratory.pdf

The Second Regional Workshop on the Enhancement of Information and Communication Technology (ICT) Accessibility for Persons with Disabilities, held on 13-15 October 2009, Annex II; available at: www.unescap.org/ ESID/Meetings/ICT09/Cam_R.pdf

UNESCO (undated) ICT and Disabled People; available at: http://portal.unesco.org/ci/en/ev.php-URL_ID =20486 &URL_ DO=DO_ PRINTPAGE &URL_ SECTION =201. html

Williams, P. et al (2007) ICTs and learning disability: multidisciplinary perspectives, Aslib Proceedings, 59 (1), pp. 97-112; available at: http://195.92.228.61/Insight/ viewContentItem.do;jsessionid=A28E4B0D425210 C977700F3E6397E53B? content Type= Article & hdAction = lnkhtml & contentId = 1589313 & history=false

Zagler, W.L. and Panek, P. (1999) Assisting the Facilitators – Interface Design and Telematic Support for ITBased Assistive Technology, *Technology and Disability*, No. 10, pp. 129-136.

2nd Semester

PGDRT 005: Computers, Communication and Control Systems

This course is designed to explore different methods for evaluating controls used to operate computers, communication devices and powered wheelchairs. Moreover, device features and integration factors are also addressed.

Suggested Readings

Abels, E.G. et al (1996) Factors that influence the use of electronic networks by science and engineering faculty at small institutions, Part I: Queries, *Journal of the American Society for Information Science*, 47(2), pp. 146-158.

Baker, P.R. (1985) Adoption of a computer software cataloging system at an elementary school." *School Library Media Quarterly*, 13(3/4), 208-214.

Barker, G. (2002, December 20) Computers just doing what comes naturally, *Melbourne Age*, available at: http://www.theage.com.au/articles/2002/12/20/1040174378191.html.

Bates, M.J. et al (1993) An analysis of search terminology used by humanities scholars: The Getty Online Searching Project Report, Number 1, *Library Quarterly*, 63(1), pp. 1-39.

Bebout, L. et al (1975) User studies in the humanities: a survey and a proposal, *RQ*, 15, pp. 40-44.

Berg, B.L. (1995) *Qualitative research methods for the social sciences*, 2nd edn. (Boston: Allyn and Bacon).

Berman, Y. (1996) Discussion groups on the Internet as sources of information: The case of social work, *Aslib Proceedings*, 48(2), pp. 31-36.

Brown, C.D. (2001) The role of computer-mediated communication in the research process of music scholars: an exploratory investigation, *Information Research*, 6(2) Available at: http://InformationR.net/ir/6-2/paper99.html

Brown, J. and Sime, J. (1981) A methodology for accounts, in: M. Brenner (Ed) *Social Method and Social Life* (Academic Press), pp. 159-188.

Burton, P.F. (1994) Electronic mail as an academic discussion forum, *Journal of Documentation*, 50(2), pp. 99-110.

Case, D.O. (1986) Collection and organization of written information by social scientists and humanists: A review and exploratory study, *Journal of Information Science*, 12, pp. 97-104.

Chatman, E.A. (1986) Diffusion theory: A review and test of a conceptual model in information diffusion, *Journal of the American Society for Information Science*, 37(6), pp. 377-386.

Cohen, J. (1996) Computer mediated communication and publication productivity among faculty, *Internet Research*, 6(2/3), pp. 41-63.

Crane, D. (1972) *Invisible Colleges: Diffusion of Knowledge in Scientific Communities* (Chicago: University of Chicago Press).

Davies, D.K. et al (2004) Computer-Mediated, Self-Directed Computer Training and Skill Assessment for Individuals with Mental Retardation, *Journal of Development and Physical Disabilities, 16*(1), 95-105.

Dervin, B. (1992) From the mind's eye of the user: The sense-making qualitative-quantitative methodology, In: J. D. Glazier and R. R. Powell (Eds) *Qualitative Research in Information Management* (Englewood: Libraries Unlimited).

--------and Clark, K. (1987) *ASQ: Alternative tools for information need and accountability assessments by libraries* (Sacramento, CA: The Peninsula Library System).

Eveland, J.D. (1986) Diffusion, technology transfer, and implementation: Thinking and talking about change, *Knowledge: Creation, Diffusion, Utilization*, 8(2), pp. 303-322.

Gould, C. (1988) *Information Needs in the Humanities: An Assessment* (Stanford, Calif.: Research Libraries Group).

Lazinger, S.S. et al (1997) Internet use by faculty members in various disciplines: A comparative case study, *Journal of the American Society for Information Science*, 48(6), pp. 508-518.

Kaminer, N. (1997) Scholars and the use of the Internet, *Library and Information Science Research*, 19, pp. 329-345.

Lönnqvist, H. (1990) Scholars seek information: Information-seeking behaviour and information needs of humanities scholars, *International Journal of Information and Library Research*, 2(3), pp. 195-203.

Marshall, J.G. (1990) Diffusion of innovation theory and end-user searching, *Library and Information Science Research*, 12, pp. 55-69.

Miles, M.B., and Huberman, M.(1984) *Qualitative Data Analysis: A Sourcebook of New Methods* (Beverly Hills: Sage Publications).

Moore, G.C., and Benbasat, I. (1991) Development of an instrument to measure the perceptions of adopting an information technology innovation, *Information Systems Research*, 2(3), 1991, pp. 192-222.

Morasso, P. et al (1979) *Towards Standardization of Communication and Control Systems for Motor Impaired People* (Berlin; Springer),17 (4), pp.

Morton, H.C., and Price, A.J. (1989) *ACLS Survey of Scholars: A Final Report of Views on Publications, Computers, and Libraries* (Washington, D.C.: American Council of Learned Societies).

O'Sullivan, E. and Rassel, G.R. (1995) *Research Methods for Public Administrators* (White Plains, NY: Longman).

Pandit, I. (1992) *'Informal Communication in the Humanities: A Qualitative Inquiry'*, unpublished doctoral dissertation (Urbana-Champaign: University of Illinois at Urbana-Champaign).

Pao, M.L. (1982) Collaboration in computational musicology, *Journal of the American Society for Information Science*, 33(1), pp. 38-43.

Peek, R.P. (1997) *Early Use of Worldwide Electronic Mailing Lists by Social Science and Humanities Scholars in the United States*, unpublished doctoral dissertation (New York: Syracuse University).

Rogers, E.M. (1995) *Diffusion of Innovations*, 4th ed. (New York: The Free Press).

Rosenbaum, H. and Snyder, H. (1991) An investigation of emerging norms in computer mediated communication: An empirical study of computer conferencing, *Proceedings of the ASIS Annual Meeting*, Washington, DC: 28, pp. 15-23.

Ruth, S.R., and Gouet, R. (1993) Must invisible colleges be invisible? An approach to examining large communities of network users, *Internet Research*, 3(1), pp. 36-51.

Schaefermeyer, M.T., and Sewell, E. H. (1988) Communicating by electronic mail, *American Behavioral Scientist*, 32, pp. 112-123.

Stephen, T., and Harrison, T.M. (1994) Comserve, moving the communication discipline online, *Journal of the American Society for Information Science*, 45(10), pp. 765-770.

Strauss, A., and Corbin, J. (1990) *Basics of Qualitative Research: Grounded Theory Procedures and Techniques* (Newbury Park, CA: Sage).

Tibbo H. (1991) Information systems, services and technology for the humanities, *Annual Review of Information Science and Technology* 26, pp. 287-346.

Tornatsky, L.G., and Klein, K.J. (1982) Innovation characteristics and innovation adoption-implementation: A meta-analysis of findings, *IEEE Transactions on Engineering Management*, 29(1), pp. 28-45.

UNESCO (2009) eAccessibility ICT and Marginalised Youth (Geneva: Communication & Information Sector; available at: http://www.epractice.eu/en/library/300042.

Weedman, J. (1993) On the "isolation" of humanists, *Communication Research*, 20(6), pp. 749-776.

Wiberley, S.E. (1991) Habits of humanists: Scholarly behavior and new information technologies, *Library Hi Tech*, 9(1), pp. 17-21.

PGDRT 006: Adaptive Equipment Design and Fabrication

This course covers design theories, idea generation, fabrication machines and hand tool techniques. Appropriate materials are also covered related to custom design and custom fabrication of low-tech adaptive equipment. Students work in the rehabilitation technology units/and other rehabilitation workshops during practice sessions, and in completing an individual project based on actual consumer request.

Suggested Readings

Bacchi, C. and Beasley, C. (2005) Reproductive technology and the political limits of care, In: Margrit Shildrick and Roxanne Mykitiuk (Eds) *Ethics of the Body: Post-conventional Challenges* (Cambridge: The MIT Press), pp. 175-94.

Batavia, A. and Hammer, G. (1990) Toward the Development of Consumer-Based Criteria for the Evaluation of Assistive Devices, *Journal of Rehabilitation Research,* 27(4), pp. 425-436.

Cook, A. M. and Hussey, S. M. (1995) *Assistive Technologies: Principles and Practice* (St. Louis, MO: Mosby Year Book).

Day, H. and Jutai, J. (1996) Measuring the Psychosocial Impact of Assistive Devices: The PIADS, *Canadian Journal of Rehabilitation,* 9, pp. 159-168.

Dell Orto, A.E. and Power, P. W. (Eds) (2007) *The Psychological and Social Impact of Illness and Disability,* 5th edn. (New York: Springer Publishing Company).

--------and Marinelli, R. P. (Eds) (1995) *Encyclopedia of Disability and Rehabilitation* (New York: Macmillan).

Eisenberg, M.G. et al (Eds) (1999) *Medical Aspects of Disability: A Handbook for the Rehabilitation Professional,* 2nd edn. (New York: Springer).

Demers, L. et al (1996) Development of the Quebec User Evaluation of Satisfaction with Assistive Technology (QUEST), *Assistive Technology,* 8, pp. 3-13.

Irvin, C. (2004) *Home Bound: Growing up with a Disability in America* (Philadelphia: Temple University Press).

O'Day, B.L. and Corcoran, P.J. (1994) Assistive Technology: Problems and Policy Alternatives, *Archives of Physical Medicine and Rehabilitation,* 75, pp. 1165-1169.

Phillips, B. and Zhao, H. (1993) Predictors of Assistive Technology Abandonment, *Assistive Technology,* 5, pp. 36-45.

Reinkensmeyer, D.J. et al (2004) Robotics, Motor Learning, and Neurologic Recovery, *Annual Review of Biomedical Engineering,* 6, pp. 497-525.

Rosen, M.J. (Ed) (2002) Recollections and Perspectives, special issue of the *Journal of Rehabilitation Research and Development,* 39(6); available at: www.vard.org/jour/02/39/6/sup/contents.html

Webster, J.G. et al (Eds) (1985) *Electronic Devices for Rehabilitation* (New York: John Wiley).

PGDRT 007: Assistive Technology for Literacy, Learning, and Participation in Pre-Primary to Higher Education

This course includes weekly hands-on lab experience along with lectures and group projects. The emphasis, however, is on learning how to use a variety of assistive technology software and techniques that can be used to make academic curriculum available for all learners. Literacy and writing software are covered extensively. Assessment techniques for diverse learners are presented.

Suggested Readings

Alessi, S.M. and Trollip, S.R. (2001) *Multimedia for Learning: Methods and Development,* 3rd edn. (Needham Heights, MA: Allyn & Bacon).

Anderson-Inman, L., and Horney, M. (1999) *Electronic books: Reading and studying with supportive resources;* available at http://www.readingonline.org/electronic/ebook.

Anderson-Inman, L. and Reinking, D. (1998) Learning from text in a post-typographic world, In: C. Hynd et al (Eds.) *Learning from Text across Conceptual Domains in Secondary Schools* (Mahwah, NJ: Lawrence Erlbaum Associates).

Behrmann, M., and Jerome, M. K. (2002) *Assistive technology for students with mild disabilities: Update 2002, ERIC Digest; available at:* http://www.ericdigests.org/2003-1/assistive.htm.

Bitter, J.A. (2000) Learner Online Interaction, *Journal of Rehabilitation Administration*, 24(1), pp. 37-45.

--------(1998)Distance Learning Considerations, *Journal of Rehabilitation Administration*, 22(2), pp. 129-135.

Blankenship, T.L. et al (2005) Effects of computer-based cognitive mapping on reading comprehension for students with emotional behavior disorders, *Journal of Special Education Technology, 20*(2).

Blaser, A. (2001) Distance Education—Boon or Bane?, *Ragged Edge Magazine*, 5, September.

Burgstahler, S. (2002) Universal Design of Distance Learning, *Information Technology and Disabilities*, (8)(1), Special Issue: Distance Education and Disability, January.

Carnevale, D. (1999) Colleges Strive to Give Disabled Students Access to On-Line Courses, *The Chronicle of Higher Education*, October 29.

Castellani, J. and Jeffs, T. (2001) Emerging reading and writing strategies using technology, *Teaching Exceptional Children*, May/June, *33*(5).

Cavalier, A. (2000) Faculty Support: Removing the Barriers to Effective Distance Education in Assistive Technology, *Technology for the New Millennium, Proceedings of the RESNA 2000 Annual Conference*, June 28-July 2 (Orlando, FL, RESNA Press, Arlington, VA). Pp. 261-263.

--------(1998) Distance Education for Postsecondary Students with Diverse Needs: The State of the Art and Science, *The State of the Arts and Science, Proceedings of the RESNA 1998 Annual Conference*, Minneapolis, MN, June 26-30, (RESNA Press, Arlington, VA), pp. 318-320.

Collins, B.C. et al (1999) So You're a Distance Learner? Tips and Suggestions for Rural Special Education Personnel Involved in Distance Education, *Rural Special Education Quarterly*, 18(3-4), pp. 66-70.

Cook, R. A. and Gladhart, M. A. (2002) A Survey of Online Instructional Issues and Strategies for Postsecondary Students with Learning Disabilities, *Information Technology and Disabilities*, (8)(1), Special Issue: Distance Education and Disability, January.

Coombs, N. (1999) Universal Access with Adaptive Technology Discussed at 14th CSUN Conference, *Library HI-Tech News*, August, 165, 13.

--------(1998) Bridging the Disability Gap with Distance Learning, *Technology and Disability*, 8(3), pp. 149-152.

Cooper, H. and Keefe, C. H. (undated) Preparation of Teachers of Visually Impaired Students via Distance Education: Perceptions of Teachers, *Journal of Visual Impairment and Blindness*, 95(9), pp. 563-566.

DeMario, N. C. and Heinze, T. (undated) The Status of Distance Education in Personnel Preparation Programs in Visual Impairment, *Journal of Visual Impairment and Blindness*, 95(9), pp. 525-532.

Englert, C.S. et al (2004) I can do it better on the computer: The effects of technology-enabled scaffolding on young writers' composition, *Journal of Special Education Technology, 19*(1).

Gallagher, P. A. and McCormick, K. (1999) Student Satisfaction with Two-Way Interactive Distance Learning for Delivery of Early Childhood Special Education Coursework, *Journal of Special Education Technology*, 14(1), pp. 32-44.

Grisham-Brown, J. et al (1998) Multi-University Collaboration via Distance Learning to Train Rural Special Education Teachers and Related Services Personnel, *Journal of Special Education Technology*, 13(4), pp. 110-121.

Hasselbring, T.S. (2001) A possible future of special education technology, *Journal of Special Education Technology, 16*(4), pp. 15-21.

Higgins, E.L. and Raskind, M. H. (1997) The compensatory effectiveness of optical character recognition/speech synthesis on reading comprehension of postsecondary students with learning disabilities, *Learning Disabilities: A Multidisciplinary Journal, 8*, pp. 75-87.

Hoenig, H. et al (2003) Does assistive technology substitute for personal assistance among the disabled elderly?, *American Journal of Public Health, 93*(2), pp. 330-337.

Huebner, K.M. and Weiner, W.R. (undated) Distance Education in 2001, *Journal of Visual Impairment and Blindness*, 95(9), pp. 517-524.

Lance, G.D. (2002) Distance Learning and Disability: A View From the Instructor's Side of the Virtual Lectern, *Information Technology and Disabilities*, (8)(1), Special Issue: Distance Education and Disability, January.

Lee, C. (1999). *Learning Disabilities and Assistive Technologies; An Emerging Way to Touch the Future* (Amherst, MA: McGowan Publications).

Liu, L. et al (2001) Evaluation of technologies for distance delivery of continuing education to rehabilitation professionals, *The AT Odyssey Continues: Proceedings of the RESNA 2001 Annual Conference*, June 22-26 (Reno, NV, RESNA Press, Arlington, VA), pp. 163-165.

Ludlow, B.L. and Brannan, S. A. (1999) Distance Education Program Preparing Personnel for Rural Areas: Current Practices, Emerging Trends, and Future Directions, *Rural Special Education Quarterly*, 18 (3-4), pp. 5-20.

Lueck, A. H. (undated) Live and Online: A Year-round Training Program for Teachers of Students with Visual Impairments in California, *Journal of Visual Impairment and Blindness*, 95(9), pp. 533-542.

MacArthur, C.A. (1996) Using technology to enhance the writing processes of students with learning disabilities, *Journal of Learning Disabilities, 29*(4), pp. 344-354.

Male, M. (1994) *Technology for Inclusion: Meeting the Special Needs of All Students* (Boston: Allyn and Bacon).

McNear, D. (2003) A Framework for Braille Literacy: Integrative Assistive Technology in the Literacy

Curriculum, Assistive Technology Application & Integration Nova Scotia ATAINS Assistive Technology 'Best Practices' Conference April 3-5.

Okolo, C.M. (2005) Interactive technologies and social studies instruction for students with mild disabilities, In: D. Edyburn et al (Eds) *The Handbook of Special Education Technology Research and Practice* (Milwaukee, WI: Knowledge by Design), pp. 623-641.

Olson, R.K. and Wise, B.W. (1992) Reading on the computer with orthographic and speech feedback, *Reading and Writing: An Interdisciplinary Journal, 4, pp.* 107-144.

Pisha, B. and Coyne, P. (2001) Smart from the Start: The Promise of Universal Design for Learning, *Remedial and Special Education*, 22(4), July/August, pp. 197-203.

Putisek, M. et al (1999) New Opportunities: Distance Learning for People with Special Needs, *Assistive Technology on the Threshold of the New Millennium, AAATE* [Association for the Advancement of Assistive Technology in Europe] *1999 Conference Proceedings*, Amsterdam, pp. 86-89.

Sargent, C.A. et al (2001) The Ohio Assistive Technology Distance Learning Project: Evolution to Web-based Education and the Implementation of an Impact Study, *The AT Odyssey Continues: Proceedings of the RESNA 2001 Annual Conference*, June 22-26 (Reno, NV, RESNA Press, Arlington, VA), pp. 208-210.

Sax, C. (1999) Distance Education: Taking It to the Next Level, *Spotlight on Technology, Proceedings of the RESNA 1999 Annual Conference*, June 25-29 (Long Beach, CA, RESNA Press, Arlington, VA), pp. 291-293.

--------(1998) Learning from a Distance: Assistive Technology Training for Rehabilitation Counselors, *The State of the Arts and Science, Proceedings of the RESNA 1998 Annual Conference*, Minneapolis, MN, June 26-30 (RESNA Press, Arlington, VA), pp. 311-313.

Scadden, L.A. (1998) The Internet and the Education of Students with Disabilities, *Technology and Disability*, 8(3), pp. 141-148.

Schenker, K.T. and Scadden, L.A. (2002) The Design of Accessible Distance Education Environments that Use Collaborative Learning, *Information Technology and Disabilities*, (8)(1), Special Issue: Distance Education and Disability, January.

Schnorr, J.M. (1999) Developing and Using Technology for Course Delivery, *Teacher and Special Education*, 22(2), pp. 114-122.

Tobin, T.J. (2002) Issues in Preparing Visually Disabled Instructors to Teach Online: A Case Study, *Information Technology and Disabilities*, (8)(1), Special Issue: Distance Education and Disability, January.

Tumlin, J. and Wolff-Heller, K. (2004) Using word prediction software to increase typing fluency with students with physical disabilities, *Journal of Special Education Technology, 19*(3).

Wood, W. M. et al (1998) Using Distance Learning to Prepare Supported Employment Professionals, *Journal of Rehabilitation*, 64(3), pp. 48-53.

PGDRT 008: Seating and Wheelchair Mobility

This course provides the student with detailed information on the issues of wheelchair seating, positioning and mobility for children and adults with physical disabilities. Emphasis is placed on evaluating for a consumer's need and identifying the appropriate technology to match those needs. Course content includes in-depth information on assessment procedures and technology selection. The student would participate in significant hands-on experiences with the technology presented as a means to understand the capabilities and potential applications. Current research related to seating and wheeled mobility is also covered throughout the course. Funding sources and associated guidelines are also covered.

Suggested Readings

Bhasin, C.A. (Determining the seating and wheeled mobility needs of clients with Multiple Sclerosis involves understanding the complex, variable nature of this disease; available at: www.wheelchairnet.org/WCN_Prodserv/Docs/.../9508art2.PDF

Boninger, M.L. et al (1997) Three-dimensional pushrim forces during two speeds of wheelchair propulsion, *Am J.Phys. Med. Rehab*; 76, pp. 420-426.

--------(1999) Wheelchair pushrim kinetics: body weight and median nerve function, *Arch Phys Med Rehab*, 80, pp. 910-5.

Dell Orto, A.E. and Power, P. W. (Eds) (2007) *The Psychological and Social Impact of Illness and Disability*, 5th edn. (New York: Springer Publishing Company).

--------and Marinelli, R. P. (Eds) (1995) *Encyclopedia of Disability and Rehabilitation* (New York: Macmillan).

Fermin, K. and Wellard, M. (undated) When seated in a wheelchair, how many degrees tilt is needed to improve postural stability for function in chidren with a neurological disorder?; available at: www.otcats.com/topics/m_wellard.pdf

Gellman, H. et al (1988) Late complications of the weight-bearing upper extremity in the paraplegic patient, *Clin Ortho Relat Rsch*, pp. 132-135.

Harrington, C. (2005) *Barrier- Free Travel: A Nuts and Bolts Guide for Wheelers and Slow Walkers—The Definitive Guide to Accessible Travel*, 2nd edn. (New York: Demos Medical Publishing).

Sie, I.H. et al (1992) Upper extremity pain in the postrehabilitation spinal cord injured patient, *Archives of Physical Medicine and Rehabilitation*, 73, pp. 44-48.

Veeger, H.E.J. et al (1989) Wheelchair propulsion technique at different speeds, *Scand J Rehab Med.*, 21, pp. 197-203.

PGDRT 009: Augmentative Communication Assessment & Development

This course covers a range of augmentative communication assessment strategies and evaluation materials utilizing case examples for discussion of specific approaches for different ages, disabilities, and settings. Special topics include vocabulary selection, communication display design, features of electronic communication aids, funding speech-generating devices, strategies for beginning communicators and partners, vision issues and the relationship between behavior and communication for individuals with complex communication needs. Students work with a wide range of speech-generating devices to conduct feature analyses of systems and to gain hands-on experience using a variety of access methods, rate enhancement techniques and vocabulary expansion tools.

Suggested Readings

Alant, E. (2005) *Intervention issues,* In: E. Alant and L.L. Lloyd (Eds) *Augmentative and Alternative Communication and Severe Disabilities: Beyond Poverty* (London, UK: Whurr), pp. 9-29.

Beukelman, D. and Mirenda, P. (2002) *Augmentative and Alternative Communication: Management of Severe Communication Disorders in Children and Adults,* 2nd edn. (Baltimore, USA: Paul H. Brookes).

Chinner, S. et al (Eds) (2001) *Developing Augmentative and Alternative Communication Policies in Schools: Information and Guidelines* (Oxford, UK: Ace Centre Advisory Trust).

Donnelly, J. (2000) Introducing Symbols to the Special Education Classroom, In: A. Wilson (Ed) *Practical Approaches to Augmentative and Alternative Communication* (Edinburgh: The CALL Centre).

Gamel-McCormick, M. and Dymond, S. (1994) *Augmentative Communications Assessment Protocol for Symbolic Augmentative Systems* (Richmond, VA: Virginia Commonwealth University).

McConkey, R. (2005) Service delivery in low- income countries, In: E. Alant and L.L. Lloyd (Eds) *Augmentative and Alternative Communication and Severe Disabilities: Beyond Poverty* (London, UK: Whurr), pp. 131-154.

Manjula, R. (2004) Overview and Current Status of Augmentative and Alternative Communication, In: M. Jayaram and R. Manjula (Eds) *Augmentative & Alternative Communication*: Proceedings of the Continuing Education Program on Augmentative and Alternative Communication (Mysore: All India Institute of Speech and Hearing).

Romski, M. and Sevcik, R. (2005) *Augmentative Communication and Early Intervention: Myths and Realities.* Infants and Young Children, 18 (3), pp. 174-185.

Proudman, A. (2007) Brief Reports towards the Development of Augmentative and Alternative Communication Practice in a Special Needs Setting in Bangalore, India, *Asia Pacific Disability Rehabilitation Journal,* 18 (2), pp. 131-145.

Siegel-Causey, E. and Guess, D. (1989) *Enhancing Nonsymbolic Communication Interactions among Learners with Severe Disabilities* (Baltimore: Paul H. Brookes).

Warrick, A. and S. Kaul (1997) *Their Manner of Speaking: Augmentative Communication for children and young adults with severe speech disorders* (Kolkata, India: Indian Institute of Cerebral Palsy).

--------(2002) *Everyone in Talking: Using Communication Displays* (Kolkata, India: Indian Institute of Cerebral Palsy).

PGDRT 010: History and Theory in the Built Environment

Explores the built environment through the Twentieth Century period. Elements of architectural theories, manifestoes, cultural literacy and self-reflection within major movements of the Twentieth Century will be explored. Among the issues to be addressed at the micro- level include Futurism, Constructivism, Functionalist Modernism, Brutalist Modernism, Rationalism, Metabolism, Eclectic Post-modernism, Neo-Classical Postmodernism, Regionalism, Late

Modernism (High-Tech), Deconstructivism/Deconstructionism, and Complexitism in architecture.

Suggested Readings

Buttimer, A. (1969) Social Space in Interdisciplinary Perspective, *Geographical Review,* 59, pp. 417-426.

Chouinard, V. (1997) Making Space for Disabling Differences: Challenging Ableist Geographies, *Environment and Planning D: Society and Space,* 15 (4), pp. 379-387.

Clapham, D. et al (1990) *Housing and Social Policy* (London: Macmillan).

Cook, A.M. and Hussey, S. M. (2002) in *Technologies That Aid Manipulation and Control of the Environment–Assistive Technologies: Principles and Practice*, 2d edn., pp. 374-408 (St. Louis, MO: C.V. Mosby).

Swain, J. et al (Eds) *Disabling Barriers– Enabling Environments (*London: Sage).

Cormode, L. (1997) Emerging Geographies of Disability and Impairment: an Introduction, *Environment and Planning D: Society and Space,* 15 (4), pp. 387-390.

Dear, M., et al (1997) Seeing People Differently: the Sociospatial Construction of Disability', *Environment and Planning D: Society and Space,* 15 (4), pp. 455-480.

Doyal, L. and Gough, I. (1991) *A Theory of Human Need* (London: Macmillan).

Gant, R. (1992) Transport for the Disabled, *Geography,* 77(1), pp. 88-91.

Gant, R. and Smith, J. (1984) 'Spatial Mobility Problems of the Elderly and Disabled in the Cotswolds', In: Clark, G. *et al*. (Eds) *The Changing Countryside, Proceedings of the First British–Dutch Symposium on Rural Geography (*Norwich: Geo Books).

--------(1991) The Elderly and Disabled in Rural Areas: Travel Patterns in the North Cotswolds, in: Champion, T. and Wadkins, C. (Eds) *People in the Countryside* (London: Paul Chapman), pp. 108-124.

Gleeson, B.J. (1995) Disability – a State of Mind?, *Australian Journal of Social Issues,* 29, 1, 10-23.

--------(1996) A Geography for Disabled People?, *Transactions, Institute of British Geographers,* 21 (2), pp. 387–396.

Grob, G.N. (1995) The Paradox of Deinstitutionalization, *Society,* July/Aug., pp. 51-59.

Hahn, H. (1986) Disability and the Urban Environment: a Perspective on Los Angeles, *Environment and Planning D: Society and Space,* 4, 273-288.

Hales, G., (ed.) (1996) *Beyond Disability: Toward an Enabling Society* (London: Sage).

Hanno-Walter Kruft (1994) *A History of Architectural Theory: From Vitruvius to the Present* (Princeton Architectural Press/PAPress).

Imrie, R.F. (1996) *Disability and the City: International Perspectives* (London: Paul Chapman).

--------(1996b) Equity, Social Justice, and Planning for Access and Disabled People: an International Perspective, *International Planning Studies,* 1(1), pp. 17-34.

Imrie, R.F. and Wells, P.E. (1993a) Disablism, Planning and the Built Environment, *Environment and Planning C: Government and Policy,* 11 (2), pp. 213-231.

--------(1993b) Creating Barrier-Free Environments, *Town and Country Planning,* 61(10), pp. 278-281.

Jaffe, M. and Smith, T.P. (1986) *Siting Homes for Developmentally Disabled Persons* (Chicago: American Planning Association).

Kridler, C. and Stewart, R.K. (1992a) Access for the Disabled 1, *Progressive Architecture,* 73 (7), pp. 41-42.

--------(1992b) Access for the Disabled 2, *Progressive Architecture,* 73 (8), pp. 35-36.

--------(1992c) Access for the Disabled 3, *Progressive Architecture,* 73 (9), pp. 45-46.

Lebovich, W.L. (1993) *Design for Dignity: Studies in Accessibility* (New York: Wiley).

Lifchez, R. and Winslow, B. (1979) *Design for Independent Living: the Environment and Physically Disabled People* (London: Architectural Press).

Wrightson, W. (1989) *From Barrier Free to Safe Environments: the New Zealand Experience* (New York: World Rehabilitation Fund).

PGDRT 011: Facilities Management: Theory and Practice

This course investigates the theory and practice of facilities management. Elements of strategic and operational facilities management will be discussed in the context of technology, cost, legal/contract, environmental and performance management. Elements of entrepreneurship will be explored in the context of facilities management business development. Among the major topics to be covered in this course include Introduction to facilities management, Strategic facilities management, Operational facilities management, Entrepreneurship and teamwork, Location and space management, Building systems maintenance management, Knowledge and information and communication technology management, Contract management, Cost management for facilities operations, Change and culture management, Disaster and security management and Performance management.

Suggested Readings

Atkin, B. and Brooks, A. (2005) *Total Facilities Management* (Wiley- Blackwell), 3rd edn.

Barrett, P. and Baldry, D. (2003) *Facilities Management* (Wiley-Blackwell), 2nd edn.

Shah, S. (2007) *Sustainable Practice for the Facilities Manager* (Wiley- Blackwell).

Booty, F. (2008) *Facilities Management Handbook* (Butterworth-Heinemann), 4th edn.

Nicolle, C. and Abascal, J. (Eds) *Inclusive Design Guidelines for HCI* (London and New York: Taylor & Francis).

Sodak, L.C. (2003) *Classroom Management in Inclusive Settings* (Wiley-Blackwell).

3rd Semester

PGDRT 012: Fieldwork/Experimentation in Disability Rehabilitation Services

This course provides experiential learning in the experiences of persons with disabilities. Students are assigned to work with and be mentored by persons with disabilities and their families. Sites would be selected in collaboration with centre or department with which the student is associated. Practicum partnerships are important as they allow students to gain valuable experience in community rehabilitation and disability studies, under the supervision of people currently working in the field. They provide students with the opportunity to learn about current issues and approaches and to apply the theory learned in their courses to professional practice.

PGDRT 013: Built Environment and Cost-Benefit Analysis

Examines the micro, macro and building economics principles relating to construction firms and industry. Elements of preliminary estimating, cost planning and application of Quantity Surveying practice will be integrated and applied to enable informed rational cost related decision-making.

Suggested Readings

Chakravarty, S.(1987) Cost-benefit analysis, *The New Palgrave: A Dictionary of Economics*, 1, pp. 687-90.

Flyvbjerg, B. et al (2002) Underestimating Costs in Public Works Projects: Error or Lie?, *Journal of the American Planning Association*, 68 (3), Summer, pp. 279-295.

Folland, S. et al (2007) *The Economics of Heath and Health Care*, 5th edn. (New Jersey: Pearson Prentice Hall), pp. 83, 84.

Frank, L.D. and Engelke, P.O. (undated) The Built Environment and Human Activity Patterns: Exploring the Impacts of Urban Form on Public Health, *Journal of Planning Literature*.

Langston, C. (2001) *Sustainable Practices in the Built Environment* (Butterworth Heinemann).

Mautone, O. (undated) The Cost Benefit Analysis and the Environment in Community Structural Funds in Italy, available at: http://www.crrconference.org/downloads/mautone1.pdf

Nas, T.F. (1996) *Cost-Benefit Analysis: Theory and Application* (Thousand Oaks, California: Sage).

Nicolle, C. and Abascal, J. (Eds) *Inclusive Design Guidelines* for HCI (London and New York: Taylor & Francis).

Thomas Barrie (2010) *The Sacred In-Between: The Mediating Roles of Architecture* (Routledge).

PGDRT 014: Internship in Rehabilitation Technology-full time

PGDRT 015: Dissertation

Students could select any topic of contemporary relevance in Disability Studies, especially with regard to rehabilitation technology, for Dissertation in consultation with their mentor/supervisor. Through the dissertation, the students could demonstrate their ability to develop and complete an in-depth analysis, select and use appropriate research methods, deploy advanced theoretical concepts and relate a focused study to broaden the scope for innovations in rehabilitation technology.

Summing Up

Disability Studies has so far been accorded recognition as a distinct academic discipline in several Western universities and academic institutions. The researchers from different professions have begun to evince keen interest in the analyses of laws, regulations and programmes affecting disabled citizens. The mounting realisation that disability must be approached from a holistic perspective has yielded a corresponding awareness that knowledge of public policies concerning disabled persons is an essential ingredient for the pursuit of such vocations.

The growth of Disability Studies as a significant field of study has been promoted both by the prior neglect of this subject in many professions and by its relevance to plethora of disciplines. Some of the specialities, which pertain to the concerns of disabled persons, have been directly or indirectly supported by governmental policies.

However, the disability policy has not yet evolved as a sub-field in several areas-such as, Rehabilitation Counselling, Special Education, Occupational/Physical Therapy, Biomedical Engineering, Medicine or Nursing Science. Other disciplines, in which linkages between disability and major theoretical paradigms could be made, have utterly failed to incorporate this area within their paradigms. Social Work, Public Health and Gerontology are worth-noting in this direction. There are other areas- such as, Architecture, Law, Business or Public Administration, and Urban or Regional Planning-requiring modification in their disciplinary orientations in response to specific policy directives. In the sphere of social sciences, probably the area of disability has been extensively researched in Psychology, Sociology, Economics and Communications. Valuable contribution could also be expected from Anthropology, Political Science, History, besides several areas of the humanities like Literature, Philosophy, Religion, and, the Arts. In addition, meaningful contribution could also be made by different streams of natural and physical sciences.

This enumeration of disciplines is quite illustrative rather than exhaustive or definitive and it should not obscure the fundamental point. An unusually wide range of academic fields could either make valuable contributions to the study of disability policy or draw heavily from such investigations. None of the existing disciplines, however, has developed research on disability policy as a major focus. These pattems have produced a wide vacuum in our country, which must be plugged especially to assist professionals (entering careers that involves extensive work with disabled persons). The field of Disability Studies is still in embryonic stage in India; as there is quite lack of planned and systematic curriculum on Disability Studies. This could well be reflected in the manner in which the courses are offered haphazardly. However, its importance and relationship to many disciplines may provide a significant explanation for seeking and anticipating the rapid expansion of this area of study.

Thus, the area of Disability Studies has become an innovative field with extensive professional and academic foundation. There is a vast and growing literature on the subject, which seems to have been largely unperused by decision makers as also researchers. Since, there is a massive population of the persons with disabilities in our country and huge amount of money has been invested so far on the rehabilitation and welfare of such disadvantaged persons under successive Five Year Plans, it could be an important area for teaching and research.

The issue of disability and the experiences of disabled people have so far been given scant consideration in academic discourses, particularly in a developing society like India. Both the issue and the experiences have been marginalised and only in certain specific disciplines, and that, too, in a rather piece-meal fashion, the area of Disability Studies has been accorded prominent place. Unfortunately, this has proved to be counter-productive with the issue of disability being visualised as essentially a medical problem and the experience of disability as being contingent upon a variety of psychological adjustment processes. In order to counter the medical and psychological dominance in this area, ultimately nothing less than a 'social theory of disability' is the need of the hour.

All these initiatives of the Government of India notwithstanding, the UGC has not taken even the first stage of constituting the Model Curriculum Development Committee on Disability Studies (as has been done in the case of Gandhian Studies, Human Rights, Dalit Studies and other academic disciplines). Meanwhile, certain universities/ academic institutions (such as, JNU, DU, IGNOU, TISS, Periyar, Alagappa, Gauhati and Ambedkar) have moved towards launching Disability Studies programmes, though in a haphazard manner because of lack of model curriculum.

The reasons for this lackadaisical attitude on the part of intelligentsia are not far to seek; as there is abysmally low level of theorization on disability and rehabilitation issues from rights-based paradigm in Indian perspectives. There is, thus, imperativeness of pedagogical development in this unexplored area in our country.

Against this background, certain pertinent questions arise: (a) What is Disability Studies and how is it related to Rehabilitation Science, Special Education, Inclusive Education, Human Rights and other academic disciplines? (b) Is it "studies" or indoctrination and who should teach it? (c) How has the curriculum of Disability Studies developed as an interdisciplinary field of academic inquiry around the globe and what implications does it have for developing countries like India? (d) Does the empowerment model enlighten us about the role of disability in the lives of individuals and society? (e) How much progress has been made in regard to development of a rights- based perspective on disability? (f) What are the historical, social and economic conditions that produce the distances and inter-relationships that exist between the "disabled" and the "normal" world? (g) How do these conditions prevent scholars from providing emancipatory model of disability research? (h) How can educators construct a curriculum so as to produce knowledges for exploring the possibility of overall material and social transformation? (i) To what extent does the informed awareness of disabled students lead to their empowerment in personal and professional lives? (j) How should the curriculum of Disability Studies be developed in Indian context in tune with rights- based approach to disability, especially in the context of India ratifying the UN Convention on the Rights of Persons with Disabilities (CRPD)?

What is urgently required is to promote teaching and research in the area of Disability Studies in universities and higher education institutions. As a first major step in this direction is to develop a Model Curriculum on Disability Studies for various programmes of studies (ranging from MA/MSc and MPhil to PhD and PG Diploma. This could go a long way in transforming the public perception about disability related issues.

There is, thus, an urgent need for various disciplines to focus attention on this neglected field of inquiry from inter-disciplinary orientations. Scholars, intellectuals and disability rights activists have onerous role to play in regard to developing the emerging field of Disability Studies from right based perspective, especially in the aftermath of ratification of UN Convention on Rights of Persons with Disabilities by the Government of India and consequently, the enactment of Rights of Persons with Disabilities Act (2016).

References

Books, Monographs & Articles/Papers

Abels, E.G. et al (1996) Factors that influence the use of electronic networks by science and engineering faculty at small institutions, Part I: Queries, *Journal of the American Society for Information Science*, 47(2), pp. 146-158.

Abend, A.C. et al (1979) *Facilities for Special Education Services: A Guide for Planning New and Renovated Schools* (Baltimore: Maryland State Department of Education).

Adams, M. and Brown, S. (Eds) (2006) *Towards Inclusive Learning in Higher Education: Developing Curricula for Disabled Students* (Oxon: Routledge).

Adams, Rachel et al (Eds) (2015) *Keywords for Disability Studies* (New York and London: New York University Press).

Adlam, T. et al (2004) The installation and support of internationally distributed equipment for people with dementia: *IEEE Transactions on Information Technology in Biomedicine*, 8 (3), pp. 253-257.

Ahmad Hassanein, Elsayed Elshabrawy (2015) *Inclusion, Disability and Culture* (Rotterdam: Sense Publishers)

Akhilnanda, C. (1952) *Mental Health and Hindu Psychology* (London: George Allen).

Albrecht, G.L. et al (Eds) (2001) *Handbook of Disability Studies* (Thousand Oaks, CA: Sage Publications).

--------(Eds) (2006) *Encyclopedia of Disability* (Thousand Oaks, CA: Sage Publications).

Albrecht, G.L. (1992) *The Disability Business: Rehabilitation in America* (Newbury Park: Sage Publications).

Alant, E. (2005) Intervention issues, In: E. Alant and L.L. Lloyd (Eds) *Augmentative and Alternative Communication and Severe Disabilities: Beyond Poverty* (London, UK: Whurr), pp. 9-29.

Alessi, S.M. and Trollip, S.R. (2001) *Multimedia for Learning: Methods and Development*, 3rd edn. (Needham Heights, MA: Allyn & Bacon).

Altman, Barbara M. (Ed) *International Measurement of Disability Purpose, Method and Application* (Switzerland: Springer)

Altman, B.M. and Barnartt, S.N. (Eds) (2006) International Views on Disability Measures: Moving toward Comparative Measurement, *Research in Social Science and Disability*, Vol. 4 (Oxford: Elsevier).

Alur, M. and Rioux, M. (2000) *Included: An Exploration of Six Early Education Pilot Projects for Children with Disabilities in India* (UNICEF, South Asia Regional Office, India, 2000).

Alvarez, Eduardo (undated) Pathways to Accessibility: Disability and the Physical Environment in Latin America and the Caribbean; available at: http://www. iadb.org/sds/ doc/Rev2bEdited Disability%2 D In fras tructureAlvarez.pdf

Anderberg, P. (2006) FACE: Disabled People, Technology and Internet (Lund University: Division of Rehabilitation Engineering Research/Department of Design Sciences), Doctoral Thesis CERTEC: LTH, No. 1.

Anderson-Inman, L., and Horney, M. (1999). *Electronic books: Reading and studying with supportive resources;* available at http://www.readingonline.org/electronic/ebook.

Anderson-Inman, L. and Reinking, D. (1998) Learning from text in a post-typographic world, In: C. Hynd et al (Eds.) *Learning from Text across Conceptual Domains in Secondary Schools* (Mahwah, NJ: Lawrence Erlbaum Associates).

Annapurna, M. (1997) *Mentally Handicapped Children and Family Stress* (New Delhi: Discovery Publishing House).

Ansley, J. (2000) *Creating Accessible Schools* (Washington, D.C.: National Clearinghouse for Educational Facilities); available at: http://www.edfacilities.org

Anthony, M, J. (1999) *Rights of Persons with Disabilities* (New Delhi: Indian Social Institute, New Delhi, 1999).

Aparna, M. (2008) ICT for Disability, M. Tech. Dissertation (Mumbai: Department of Computer Science and Engineering, Indian Institute of Technology, Bombay).

Armstrong, F. and Barton, L. (Eds) (2000) *Disability, Human Rights, and Education: Cross-Cultural Perspectives* (Sheffield, UK: Open University Press).

Arneil, Barbara and Hirschman, Nancy J. (Eds) (2016) *Disability and Political Theory* (Cambridge: Cambridge University Press)

Asch, Adrienne and Mccarthy, Henry (n.d.) Infusing Disability Studies into Psychology Curriculum, available at: file:///C:/Users/sfd/Downloads/Infusing%20Disability%20Issues%20into%20Psychology.pdf

Aspinall, A. and Hegarty, J. R. (2001) ICT for adults with learning disabilities: An organisationwide audit, *British Journal of Educational Technology, 32*(3), pp. 365-372.

Atkin, B. and Brooks, A. (2005) *Total Facilities Management* (Wiley-Blackwell), 3rd edn.

Awasthi, S.K. (2000) *Rights of Unsound Mind Accused* (Pune: C T J Publication).

Babbitt, B. et al (2002) The movement of accessible design principles into mainstream engineering: Now and then, In: J.M. Winters et al (Eds) *Emerging and Accessible Telecommunications, Information and Healthcare Technologies (RESNA Press), pp. 2-18).*

Bacchi, C. and Beasley, C. (2005) Reproductive technology and the political limits of care, In: Margrit Shildrick and Roxanne Mykitiuk (Eds) *Ethics of the Body: Postconventional Challenges* (Cambridge: The MIT Press), pp. 175-94.

Baglieri, S. et al (2006) *Engaging in Disability Studies Research: An Autoethnographic Exploration,* presented at the American Educational Research Association's 2006 annual meeting at San Francisco, CA.

Baker, P.R. (1985) Adoption of a computer software cataloging system at an elementary school." *School Library Media Quarterly*, 13(3/4), 208-214.

Balen, R. and Crawshaw (Eds) (2006) *Sexuality and Fertility Issues in Ill Health and Disability: From Early Adolescence to Adulthood* (London: Jessica Kingsley Publishers).

Barker, G. (2002, December 20) Computers just doing what comes naturally, *Melbourne Age*, available at: http://www.theage.com.au/articles/2002/12/20/1040174378191.html.

Batavia, A. and Hammer, G. (1990) Toward the Development of Consumer-Based Criteria for the Evaluation of Assistive Devices, *Journal of Rehabilitation Research*, 27(4), pp. 425-436.

Bates, M.J. et al (1993) An analysis of search terminology used by humanities scholars: The Getty Online Searching Project Report, Number 1, *Library Quarterly*, 63(1), pp. 1-39.

Bebout, L. et al (1975) User studies in the humanities: a survey and a proposal, *RQ*, 15, pp. 40-44.

Berg, B.L. (1995) *Qualitative research methods for the social sciences*, 2nd edn. (Boston: Allyn and Bacon).

Berman, Y. (1996) Discussion groups on the Internet as sources of information: The case of social work, *Aslib Proceedings*, 48(2), pp. 31-36.

Booty, F. (2008) *Facilities Management Handbook* (Butterworth-Heinemann), 4th edn.

Brown, C.D. (2001) The role of computer-mediated communication in the research process of music scholars: an exploratory investigation, Information Research, 6(2) Available at: http://InformationR.net/ir/6-2/paper99.html

Brown, J. and Sime, J. (1981) A methodology for accounts, in: M. Brenner (Ed) *Social Method and Social Life* (Academic Press), pp. 159-188.

Burton, P.F. (1994) Electronic mail as an academic discussion forum, *Journal of Documentation*, 50(2), pp. 99-110.

Barnartt, S. and Scotch, R.(2001) *Disability Protests: Contentious Politics, 1970-1999* (Washington, DC: Gallaudet University Press).

Bartlett, P. et al (2007) *Mental Disability and the European Convention on Human Rights* (Leiden/Boston: Martinus Nijhoff Publishers).

Barnes, C. and Mercer, G. (Eds) (2002) *Disability Studies Today* (Cambridge: Polity Press).

--------et al (Eds)(1999) *Exploring Disability: A Sociological Introduction* (Cambridge: Polity Press).

Barnes, C. (2000) A working social model? disability, work and disability politics in the 21st Century, *Critical Social Policy*, 20 (4), pp. 441-457.

Barnes, C. and Mercer, G. (2003) *Disability* (Oxford: Polity Press).

--------et al (Eds)(1999) *Exploring Disability: A Sociological Introduction* (Cambridge: Polity Press).

Barnes, C. and Mercer G.(1997) *Doing Disability Research* (Leeds: The Disability Press).

Barnes, C. (1992) *Disabling Imagery and the Media* (Halifax: Ryburn and British Council of Disabled People).

Barnes, Elizabeth (Ed) (2016) *The Minority Body : A Theory of Disability* (OUP)

Barrett, P. and Baldry, D. (2003) *Facilities Management* (Wiley-Blackwell), 2nd edn.

Barton, L. and Oliver, M. (Eds) (1997) *Disability Studies: Past, Present and Future* (Leeds: The Disability Press).

Barton, L. (Ed) (2005) *Disability and Dependency* (East Sussex: The Falmer Press).

Barton, L. and Armstrong, F. (Eds) (2008) *Policy, Experience and Change: Cross-Cultural Reflections on Inclusive Education* (London: Springer).

Bates, R. and Jones, M. (2003) Using Computer Software to Develop Switch Skills, *Technology and Persons with Disabilities,Conference Proceedings; retrieved at:* http://www.csun.edu/cod/conf/2003/proceedings/6.htm.

Baylies, C (2002) Disability and the notion of human development: questions of rights and capabilities, *Disability and Society*, 17(7), pp. 725-739.

Beauchamp-Pryor, Karen et al (Eds)(2013) *Purpose, Process and Future Direction of Disability Research* (Rotterdam: Sense Publishers).

Behrmann, M. and Schaff, J. (2001) Assisting educators with assistive technology: Enabling children to achieve independence in living and learning, *Children and Families* 42(3), pp. 24-28.

Beukelman, D. and Mirenda, P. (2002) *Augmentative and Alternative Communication: Management of Severe Communication Disorders in Children and Adults, 2nd* edn. (Baltimore, USA: Paul H. Brookes).

Bishop, J. (2003) The Internet for educating individuals with social impairments, *Journal of Computer Assisted Learning*, 19(4), 546-556.

Becker, G. (1994) The Oldest Old: Autonomy in the Face of Frailty, *Journal of Aging Studies* 8(1), pp. 59-76.

Beckett, A. E. (2006) *Citizenship and Vulnerability: Disability and Issues of Social and Political Engagement* (Houndmills: Palgrave Macmillan).

Behrmann, M. and Schaff, J. (2001) Assisting educators with assistive technology: Enabling children to achieve independence in living and learning, *Children and Families*, 42(3), pp. 24-28.

Behrmann, M., and Jerome, M.K. (2002) *Assistive technology for students with mild disabilities: Update 2002, ERIC Digest; available at:* http://www.ericdigests.org/2003-1/assistive.htm.

Bennett, J. et al (2002) *Rehabilitation Engineering Research Center on Recreational Technologies and Exercise Physiology Benefiting Persons with Disabilities (REC-TEC).*

Benson, B.L. et al (1981) *Solutions for problems of visually-impaired users of rail rapid transit. Volume 1 of: Improving communications with the visually impaired in rail rapid transit systems* (Washington, DC: U.S. Department of Transportation).

Berkowitz, M. et al (1976) *Public Policy toward Disability* (New York: Preager).

--------and M. Anne Hill (Eds) (undated) *Disability and the Labour Market: Economic Problems, Policies and Programs* (Ithaca, NY: ILR Press).

Best, S. (2005) *Understanding Social Divisions* (London: Sage Publications Limited).

Bhasin, C.A. (Determining the seating and wheeled mobility needs of clients with Multiple Sclerosis involves understanding the complex, variable nature of this disease; available at: www.wheelchairnet.org/WCN_Prodserv/Docs/.../9508art2.PDF

Bickenbach, J. (2001) Disability human rights law and policy, In: G.L. Albrecht et al (Eds) *Handbook of Disability Studies* (Thousand Oaks, California: Sage Publications).

Bishop, J. (2003) The Internet for educating individuals with social impairments, *Journal of Computer Assisted Learning*, 19(4), pp. 546-556.

Bitter, J.A. (2000) Learner Online Interaction, *Journal of Rehabilitation Administration*, 24(1), pp. 37-45.

--------(1998) Distance Learning Considerations, *Journal of Rehabilitation Administration*, 22(2), pp. 129-135.

Blanck, Peter and Flynn, ilionóir (Eds) (2017) *Routledge Handbook of Disability Law and Human Rights* (London and New York: Routledge).

Blanck, Peter (Ed) (2005) *Disability Rights* (Aldershot: Ashgate Publishing Limited).

Blankenship, T.L. et al (2005) Effects of computer-based cognitive mapping on reading comprehension for students with emotional behavior disorders, *Journal of Special Education Technology, 20*(2).

Blaser, A. (2001) Distance Education—Boon or Bane?, *Ragged Edge Magazine*, 5, September.

Blischak, D.M. and Schlosser, R. W. (2003) Use of technology to support independent spelling by students with autism, *Topics in Language Disorders, 23*(4), pp. 293-304.

Blustein, D.L. (2006) *The Psychology of Working* (Mahwah, NJ: Lawrence Erlbaum Associates Publishers).

Bode, B.H. (1937) *Modern Education Theories* (New York: The MacMillan Company).

Bodine, Cathy (2013) *Assistive Technology and Science* (Los Angeles: Sage).

Boissevain, G.W.O. and Prins, M. (1995) Architectural management and design management - the state of the art in Netherlands and ideas for research, *International Journal of Architectural Management, Practice and Research*, 9.

Bond, T. (2008) *Standards and Ethics for Counselling in Action* (London: Sage publications).

Boninger, M.L. et al (1997) Three-dimensional pushrim forces during two speeds of wheelchair propulsion, *Am J Phys Med Rehab*, 76, pp. 420-426.

--------(1999) Wheelchair pushrim kinetics: body weight and median nerve function, *Arch Phys Med Rehab*, 80, pp. 910-5.

Bortz, W.M. (2002) A Conceptual Framework of Frailty: A Review, *Journals of Gerontology Series A: Biological Sciences and Medical Sciences*, 57a(5), pp. 283-289.

Bourke, A. et al (1998) Universal instruction design in higher education: An approach for inclusion, *Equity & Excellence in Education, 31*(2), pp. 47-51.

Braddock, D. (2004) *Emerging Technologies and Cognitive Disability, Journal of Special Education Technology*, 19(4), fall; available at: http://www.colemaninstitute.org/article_braddock_1.pdf

Braddock, D.L. and Parish, S.L. (2001) An Institutional History of Disability, In: Gary L. Albrecht et al (Eds) *Handbook of Disability Studies* (Thousand Oaks, CA: Sage), pp. 11-68.

Bragg, L. (1997) From the mute God to the lesser God: disability in medieval Celtic and Old Norse literature,*Disability & Society*,12,pp.165-177.

Brail, R., Hughes, J. and Arthur, C. (1976) *Transportation Services for the Disabled and Elderly (*New Brunswick, NJ: Center for Urban Policy and Research).

Bright, K. and Giulio, R. D. (undated) *Inclusive Buildings: Designing and Managing Accessible Environments* (Blackwell Science).

Brown, S.C. (2001) Methodological Paradigms that Shape Disability Research, In: Gary L. Albrecht et al (Eds) *Disability Studies Handbook.* (Thousand Oaks, CA: Sage), pp. 145-70.

Bruyère, S.M. et al (2006) Information technology (IT) accessibility: Implications for employment of people with disabilities, *Work: A Journal of Prevention, Assessment and Rehabilitation*, 27 (4).

Bryan, W.V. (2006) *In Search of Freedom: How persons with disabilities have been disenfranchised from the mainstream of American Society and how the search for freedom continues* (Springfield, Illinois: Charles C. Thomas Publisher Limited).

--------(2007) Multicultural Aspects of Disabilities: A Guide to Understanding and Assisting Minorities in the Rehabilitation Process (Springfield, Illinois: Charles C. Thomas Publisher Ltd.).

Bucks, Christa (Ed) (1997) *A World of Options: A Guide to International Exchange, Travel, and Community Service for Persons with Disabilities,* 3d ed. (Eugene, OR: Mobility International).

Burgstahler, S. (2002) Universal Design of Distance Learning, *Information Technology and Disabilities,* (8)(1), Special Issue: Distance Education and Disability, January.

Burns, R.B. (2000) *Introduction to Research Methods* (London: Sage).

Butler, R. and Parr, H. (Eds) (2005) *Mind and Body Space: Geographies of Illness, Impairment and Disability* (London and New York: Routledge).

Buttimer, A. (1969)Social Space in Interdisciplinary Perspective, *Geographical Review*, 59, pp. 417-426.

Cain, S. (2001) *Accessing Technology- Using Technology to Support the Learning and employment Opportunities for Visually Impaired Users* (London: Royal National Institute for the Blind).

Calderón-Almendros, Ignacio and Habegger-Lardoeyt, Sabina (2017) *Education, Disability and Inclusion: A Family Struggle against an Excluding School* (Rotterdam: Sense Publishers)

Campbell, J. and Oliver, M.(1996) *Disability Politics: Understanding our Past, Changing our Future* (London and New York: Routledge).

Carcopino, J. (1940) *Daily Life in Ancient Rome: The People and Their City at the Height of the Empire* (New Haven, CT: Yale University Press).

Carnevale, D. (1999) Colleges Strive to Give Disabled Students Access to On-Line Courses, *The Chronicle of Higher Education*, October 29.

Case, D.O. (1986) Collection and organization of written information by social scientists and humanists: A review and exploratory study, *Journal of Information Science*, 12, pp. 97-104.

Castellani, J. and Jeffs, T. (2001) Emerging reading and writing strategies using technology, *Teaching Exceptional Children*, May/June, *33*(5).

Cavalier, A. (2000) Faculty Support: Removing the Barriers to Effective Distance Education in Assistive Technology, *Technology for the New Millennium, Proceedings of the RESNA 2000 Annual Conference*, June 28-July 2 (Orlando, FL, RESNA Press, Arlington, VA). Pp. 261-263.

--------(1998) Distance Education for Postsecondary Students with Diverse Needs: The State of the Art and Science, *The State of the Arts and Science, Proceedings of the RESNA 1998 Annual Conference,* Minneapolis, MN, June 26-30, (RESNA Press, Arlington, VA), pp. 318-320.

Chakravarty, S.(1987) Cost-benefit analysis, *The New Palgrave: A Dictionary of Economics,* 1, pp. 687-90.

Charema, J. and Ngazimbi, E. E. (undated) The Approaches used in Counseling Parents of Children with Disabilities in the Western and African Tradition With Particular Emphasis to Zimbabwe, available at: http://www.ohiocounseling.org/docs/JA/John_Charema_Ohio_Final_4-05-09.pdf

Charlton, J.I. (1998) *Nothing about us without us: Disability Oppression and Empowerment* (Berkeley: University of California Press).

Chater, K. (2002) Aging: A Body of Resistance, *Nursing and Health Sciences,* 4(3), pp. 123-130.

Chatman, E.A. (1986) Diffusion theory: A review and test of a conceptual model in information diffusion, *Journal of the American Society for Information Science,* 37(6), pp. 377-386.

Chew, K.A., and Manzer, D. (1986) Light rail or light rapid transit in Western Canada: A lesson planning aid, paper presented at the International Conference on the Visually Impaired Traveller in Mass Transit - Issues in Orientation and Mobility.

Chinner, S. et al (Eds) (2001) *Developing Augmentative and Alternative Communication Policies in Schools: Information and Guidelines* (Oxford, UK: Ace Centre Advisory Trust).

Chouinard, V. (1997) Making Space for Disabling Differences: Challenging Ableist Geographies, *Environment and Planning D: Society and Space,* 15 (4), pp. 379-387.

Cincotti, F. (2008) Research report: Non-invasive brain-computer interface system: Towards its application as assistive technology, *Brain Research Bulletin,* 75, pp. 796-803.

Clapham, D. et al (1990) *Housing and Social Policy* (London: Macmillan).

Clare, E. (1999) *Exile & pride: Disability, queerness, and liberation* (Cambridge, MA: South End Press).

Clarke, K. et al (2003) Designing acceptable 'smart' home technology to support people in the home, *Technology and Disability, 15*(3), pp. 191-199.

Clements, L. and Read, J. (Eds) (2008) *Disabled Peoiple and the Right to Life: The Protection and Violation Disabled People's Most Most Basic Human Rights* (Oxon: Routledge).

Cohen, J. (1996) Computer mediated communication and publication productivity among faculty, *Internet Research*, 6(2/3), pp. 41-63.

Collins, B.C. et al (1999) So You're a Distance Learner? Tips and Suggestions for Rural Special Education Personnel Involved in Distance Education, *Rural Special Education Quarterly*, 18(3-4), pp. 66-70.

Connor, David J. et al (Eds) (2014) *Practicing Disability Studies in Education: Acting Toward Social Change* (New York: Peter Lang Publishing)

Cook, R.A. and Gladhart, M.A. (2002) A Survey of Online Instructional Issues and Strategies for Postsecondary Students with Learning Disabilities, *Information Technology and Disabilities*, (8)(1), Special Issue: Distance Education and Disability, January.

Cook, A. and Hussey, S. (2002) *Assistive Technologies- Principles and Practice*, 2nd Edition (Mosby).

Cook, A.M. and Hussey, S.M. (1995) *Assistive Technologies: Principles and Practice* (St. Louis, MO: Mosby Year Book).

Cook, A.M. and Hussey, S.M. (2002) *Technologies That Aid Manipulation and Control of the Environment —Assistive Technologies: Principles and Practice*, 2nd edn., pp. 374-408 (St. Louis, MO: C.V. Mosby).

Coombs, N. (1999) Universal Access with Adaptive Technology Discussed at 14th CSUN Conference, *Library HI-Tech News*, August, 165, 13.

--------(1998) Bridging the Disability Gap with Distance Learning, *Technology and Disability*, 8(3), pp. 149-152.

Cooper, H. and Keefe, C. H. (undated) Preparation of Teachers of Visually Impaired Students via Distance Education: Perceptions of Teachers, *Journal of Visual Impairment and Blindness*, 95(9), pp. 563-566.

Cooper, M. (1990) *Women and Disability* (Canberra: Disabled People's International).

Corcoran, Tim et al (Eds) (2015) *Disability Studies: Educating for Inclusion* (Rotterdam: Sense Publishers).

Corey, G. (2001) *Theory and Practice of Counselling and Psychotherapy*, 6th edn. (Pacific Grove, Brooks Cole).

Corker, M. and French, S. (Eds) (1999) *Disability Discourse* (Milton Keynes: Open University Press), pp. 129-35

Corker, M. and Shakespeare, T. (Eds) (2002) *Disability/ Postmodernity: Embodying Disability Theory* (New York: Continuum).

Cormode, L. (1997) Emerging Geographies of Disability and Impairment: an Introduction, *Environment and Planning D: Society and Space*, 15 (4), pp. 387-390

Corn, A., and Zachs, S.Z. (1994) The impact of non-driving on adults with visual impairments, *Journal of Vision Impairment and Blindness*, Jan-Feb, pp. 53-68.

Crane, D. (1972) *Invisible Colleges: Diffusion of Knowledge in Scientific Communities* (Chicago: University of Chicago Press).

Couser, G.T. (1997) *Recovering Bodies: Illness, Disability, and Life Writing* (Madison, WI: University of Wisconsin Press).

Cresswell, J.A. (2002) *Research Design: Qualitative, Quantitative and Mixed Methods Approaches* (London, Sage publications).

Crosling, G. et al (Eds) (2008) *Improving Student Retention in Higher Education* (London and New York: Routledge).

Cross, M. (1999) Accessing the Inaccessible: Disability and Archaeology, *Archaeological Review from Cambridge*, 15(2), pp. 7-30.

Crutchfield, S. and Epstein, M. (Eds) (2000) *Points of Contact: Disability, Art, and Culture (*Ann Arbor: University of Michigan Press).

Danford, G.S. and Tauke, B. (Eds) (2002) *Universal Design (New York).*

Danforth, S. and Gabel, S. L. (Eds) (2006) *Vital Questions facing Disability Studies in Education* (New York: Peter Lang).

Dario, P. et al (1999) MOVAID: A personal robot in everyday life of disabled and elderly people, *Technology and Disability, 10*(2), pp. 77-93.

Dasen, V. (1995) *Dwarfs in Ancient Egypt and Greece* (Oxford, UK: Clarendon).

Davenport, R. et al (2003) Assistive environments for successful aging, In: M. Mokhtari (Ed) Independent living for persons with disabilities and elderly people, 1st International Conference on Smart Homes and Health Telematics, Assistive Techology Research Series (IOS Press), 12, pp. 104-110.

Davies, D.K. et al (2003) Utilization of Computer Technology to Facilitate Money Management by Individuals with Mental Retardation, *Education and Training in Mental Retardation and Developmental Disabilities, 38*(1), pp. 106-112.

Davies, D.K. et al (2004) Computer-Mediated, Self-Directed Computer Training and Skill Assessment for Individuals with Mental Retardation, *Journal of Development and Physical Disabilities, 16*(1), 95-105.

Davis, L. J. (Ed.) (2014) *The Disability Studies Reader* (New York: Routledge).

Davis, L. (1995) *Enforcing Normalcy: Disability, Deafness, and the Body* (New York: Verso).

Davis, L. and Linton, S. (1995) Disability Studies [Feature issue], *Radical Teacher,* fall, No. 47.

Day, H. and Jutai, J. (1996) Measuring the Psychosocial Impact of Assistive Devices: The PIADS, *Canadian Journal of Rehabilitation,* 9, pp. 159-168.

Dear, M., et al (1997) Seeing People Differently: the Sociospatial Construction of Disability', *Environment and Planning D: Society and Space*, 15 (4), pp. 455-480.

Degener, Theresia (2016) Disability in a Human Rights Context, *Laws*, 5 (35), pp. 1-24

Dell Orto, A. E. and Power, P. W. (Eds) (2007) *The Psychological and Social Impact of Illness and Disablity* (New York:Springer Publishing Company), 5th edn.

Dell Orto, A. E. and Marinelli, R. P. (Eds) (1995) *Encyclopedia of Disability and Rehabilitation* (Macmillan Library Reference USA).

DeMario, N. C. and Heinze, T. (undated) The Status of Distance Education in Personnel Preparation Programs in Visual Impairment, *Journal of Visual Impairment and Blindness*, 95(9), pp. 525-532.

Demers, L. et al (1996) Development of the Quebec User Evaluation of Satisfaction with Assistive Technology (QUEST), *Assistive Technology*, 8, pp. 3-13.

Dervin, B. (1992) From the mind's eye of the user: The sense-making qualitative-quantitative methodology, In: J. D. Glazier and R. R. Powell (Eds) *Qualitative Research in Information Management* (Englewood: Libraries Unlimited).

--------and Clark, K. (1987) *ASQ: Alternative tools for information need and accountability assessments by libraries* (Sacramento, CA: The Peninsula Library System).

Desai, A.N. (1995) *Helping the Handicapped* (New Delhi: Ashish Publishing House).

Despouy, L. (1993) *Human Rights and Disabled* (New York: United Nations).

Deutsch, H. and Nussbaum, F. (Eds) (2000) *DEFECT! Engendering the Modern Body* (Ann Arbor: University of Michigan Press).

Dewey, L. (1916, 1961) *Democracy and Education* (New York: MacMillan)

Deyer, J.W. (2005) Decoding accessible-design terms, *PN/ Paraplegia News, 59* (1), pp. 24-28.

Dhanda, A. (2000) *Legal Order and Mental Disorder* (New Delhi: Sage Publications).

Digital Angel (2002) *The Digital Angel Personal Safety and Location System with GPS Technology,* retrieved from: http://www.digitalangel.net/default.asp.

Disabled World (2018) Disability Statistics: Information, Charts, Graphs and Tables, available at: https://www.disabled-world.com/disability/statistics/

Donnelly, J. (2000) *Introducing Symbols to the Special Education Classroom,* In: A. Wilson (Ed) *Practical Approaches to Augmentative and Alternative Communication* (Edinburgh: The CALL Centre).

Douglas, G. (2002) ICT, Education, and Visual Impairment, *British Journal of Educational Technology,* 32 (3), pp. 353 - 364.

Dowling, C. (2000) *The Frailty Myth: Women Approaching Physical Equality* (New York: Random House).

Doyal, L. and Gough, I. (1991) *A Theory of Human Need* (London: Macmillan).

Drifte, C. (2004) *Encouraging Positive Behaviour in the Early Years: A Practical Guide* (London: Paul Chapman Publishing).

Drill, H. (2005) A closer look: A move toward accessible hotels, *PN/Paraplegia News, 59*(1), pp. 53-55.

Dryden, W. and Reeves, A. (2008) *Key Issues for Counselling in Action* (London: Sage Publications).

Dunn, Dana (2015) *The Social Psychology of Disability* (New York: OUP).

Ebersole, P. et al (2004) *Toward Healthy Aging: Human Needs & Nursing Response,* 6th edn. (St. Louis, MO: C.V. Mosby).

Edwards, A.D. N. (Ed.) (1995) *Extra-Ordinary Human-Computer Interaction: Interfaces for Users with Disabilities,* Cambridge Series on Human-Computer Interaction (New York, Cambridge University Press), also available as part of the CD-rom, Overcoming Barriers: Theory and Practice in Disability, Cambridge University Press, 1999).

Eisenberg, M. G. et al (Eds) (1999) *Medical Aspects of Disability: A Handbook for the Rehabilitation Professional*, 2nd edn. (New York: Springer).

Emmitt, S. (2001) Architectural management—an evolving field, *Engineering Construction and Architectural Management*, 6 (2).

--------(2007) *Design Management for Architects* (Oxford: Blackwell Publishing).

--------et al (2009) *Architectural Management: International Research and Practice* (Oxford: Wiley-Blackwell).

Englert, C.S. et al (2004) I can do it better on the computer: The effects of technology-enabled scaffolding on young writers' composition, *Journal of Special Education Technology, 19*(1).

Eveland, J.D. (1986) Diffusion, technology transfer, and implementation: Thinking and talking about change, *Knowledge: Creation, Diffusion, Utilization*, 8(2), pp. 303-322.

Falvo, D. (2005) *Medical and Psychosocial Aspects of Chronic Illness and Disability*, 3rd edn., (Boston: Jones and Bartlett Publishers).

Fawcett, B. (2000) *Feminist Perspectives on Disability* (Essex: Pearson Education Limited).

Federici, Stefano and Scherer, Marcia Joslyn (2018) *Assistive Technology Assessment Handbook* (New York: CRC Press), second edition.

Ferguson, P.M. (2001) Mapping the family: Disability Studies and the exploration of parental response to disability, In: Gary L. Albrecht et al (Eds) *Handbook of Disability Studies* (Thousand Oaks, CA: Sage), pp. 373-95.

Fermin, K. and Wellard, M. (undated) When seated in a wheelchair, how many degrees tilt is needed to improve postural stability for function in chidren with a neurological disorder?; available at: www.otcats.com/topics/m_wellard.pdf

Fine, M. and Asch, A. (1988) *Women with Disabilities: Essays in Psychology, Culture, and Politics (*Philadelphia: Temple University Press).

Finger, A. (1990) *Past Due: A Story of Disability, Pregnancy and Birth* (London: The Women's Press).

Finkelstein, V. (1980) *Attitudes and Disabled People* (New York: World Rehabilitation Fund).

Fischer, G., & Sullivan, J. (2002). *Human-Centered Public Transportation Systems for Persons with Cognitive Disabilities-Challenges and Insights for Participatory Design, a* paper presented at the Participatory Design Conference (PDC'02), Malmö University, Sweden; available at: http://www.cs.colorado.edu/~l3d/clever/assets/pdf/gf-pdc2002-mfa.pdf]

Fleischer, D.J. and Zames, F. (2001) *The Disability Rights Movement: From Charity to Confrontation* (Philadelphia: Temple University Press).

Flyvbjerg, B. et al (2002) Underestimating Costs in Public Works Projects: Error or Lie?, *Journal of the American Planning Association*, 68 (3), Summer, pp. 279-295.

Folland, S. et al (2007) *The Economics of Heath and Health Care*, 5th edn. (New Jersey: Pearson Prentice Hall), pp. 83, 84.

Frank, L.D. and Engelke, P.O. (undated) The Built Environment and Human Activity Patterns: Exploring the Impacts of Urban Form on Public Health, *Journal of Planning Literature*.

Foucault, M. (1980) *The History of Sexuality, vol.1, An Introduction* (New York: Vintage).

--------(1986) *The History of Sexuality, vol.2, The Use of Pleasure* (New York: Vintage).

--------(1988) *The History of Sexuality, vol.3, The Care of the Self* (New York: Vintage).

Frank, G. (2000) *Venus on Wheels: Two Decades of Dialogue on Disability, Biography and Being Female in America* (Berkeley and Los Angeles, California: University of California Press).

Franklin, K.S. (1991) Supported employment and assistive technology-A powerful partnership, In: S. L. Griffin and

W.G. Revell (Eds) *Rehabilitation Counselor Desktop Guide to Supported Employment* (Richmond, VA: Virginia Commonwealth University Rehabilitation Research and Training Center on Supported Employment).

Fraser, Benjamin (Ed) (2016) *Cultures of Representation: Disability in World Cinema Contexts* (London: Wallflower Press).

French, Sally and Swain, John (2008) *Understanding Disability. A Guide for Health Professionals* (Philadelphia: Churchill Livingstone Elsevier).

Friedman, H.S. (Ed) (2001) *The Disorders: Specialty Articles from the Encyclopedia of Mental Health* (San Diego: Academic Press).

Gabel, S. (Ed) (2005) *Disability Studies in Education: Readings in Theory and Method* (New York: Peter Lang).

Gallagher, P.A. and McCormick, K. (1999) Student Satisfaction with Two-Way Interactive Distance Learning for Delivery of Early Childhood Special Education Coursework, *Journal of Special Education Technology*, 14(1), pp. 32-44.

Gallagher, D.J. et al (2004) *Challenging Orthodoxy in Special Education: Dissenting Voices* (Denver: Love Publishing Company).

Galvin, J.C.· and McLaurin, C.A. (1991) A History of Rehabilitation Engineering, *REHAB Management*, August/ September, pp. 70-77.

Gamel-McCormick, M. and Dymond, S. (1994) *Augmentative Communications Assessment Protocol for Symbolic Augmentative Systems* (Richmond, VA: Virginia Commonwealth University).

Gant, R. and Smith, J. (1984) 'Spatial Mobility Problems of the Elderly and Disabled in the Cotswolds', In: Clark, G. *et al.* (Eds) *The Changing Countryside, Proceedings of the First British–Dutch Symposium on Rural Geography* (Norwich: Geo Books).

--------(1991) The Elderly and Disabled in Rural Areas: Travel Patterns in the North Cotswolds, in: Champion, T. and Wadkins, C. (Eds) *People in the Countryside* (London:Paul Chapman), pp. 108-124.

Gant, R. (1992) Transport for the Disabled, *Geography*, 77(1), pp. 88-91.

Garland, R. (1995) *The Eye of the Beholder: Deformity & Disability in the Graeco-Roman World* (Ithaca, NY: Cornell University Press).

Garland-Thomson, R. (1994) Redrawing the boundaries of feminist Disability Studies, *Feminist Disability Studies*, 20(3), 583-597.

Gärling, T. et al (1994) Computational-process modelling of household activity scheduling, *Transportation Research* (in press).

Gartner, A. and Joe, T. (Eds) (1987) *Images of the Disabled, Disabling Images* (New York: Praeger).

Gawali, G. (2007) Sexuality of women with disabilities: psycho- social issues, *International Journal of Disability Studies*, special issue on 'Disability, Sexuality and Human Rights', 3 (1 & 2), Jan.-Dec., pp. 35-51.

Gellman, H. et al (1988) Late complications of the weight-bearing upper extremity in the paraplegic patient, *Clin. Ortho. Relat. Rsch*; pp. 132-135.

Gerber, D. (2000) *Disabled Veterans in History* (Ann Arbor: Univ. of Michigan Press).

Ghai, A. (2007) Some observations on sexual empowerment of disabled women in India, *International Journal of Disability Studies*, special issue on 'Disability, Sexuality and Human Rights', 3 (1 & 2), Jan. - Dec., pp. 26-34.

Ghai, A. (2007) *(Dis)embodied Form: Issues of Disabled Women* (New Delhi: Har Anand Publications).

--------(2002) Disabled women: An excluded agenda of Indian feminism, *Hypatia*, 17(3), pp. 49-66.

Ghosh, A. (2007) Women with disabilities and sexual and Reproductive health with special reference to HIV/ AIDS, *International Journal of Disability Studies*, special issue on 'Disability, Sexuality and Human Rights', 3 (1 & 2), Jan.- Dec., pp. 52-68.

Gilliland, J. and Bowman (2003) *Theories and Strategies in Counseling and Psychotherapy*, 5th ed. (Boston: Allyn and Bacon).

Gitlin, L. (1995) Why Older People Accept or Reject Assistive Technology, *Generations* (Spring), pp. 41–46.

Gleeson, B. (2005) Can technology overcome the disabling city?, In: R. Butler and Hester Parr (Eds) (2005) *Mind and Body Space: Geographies of Illness, Impairment and Disability* (London and New York: Routledge).

--------(1999) *Geographies of Disability* (New York: Routledge).

--------(1995) Disability – a State of Mind?, *Australian Journal of Social Issues*, 29, 1, 10-23.

--------(1996) A Geography for Disabled People?, *Transactions, Institute of British Geographers*, 21 (2), pp. 387-396.

Goffman, E. (1963) *Stigma: Notes on the Management of Spoiled Identity* (New York: Touchstone).

Golledge, R.G. et al (1995) Public Transit Use by Non-Driving Disabled Persons: the Case of the Blind and Vision Impaired, paper prepared for the Annual PATH Conference, Richmond Field Station, October 13; available at: http://www.path.berkeley.edu/path/publications/pdf/PWP/96/PWP-96-01.pdf

--------et al (1991) Designing a personal guidance system to aid navigation without sight: Progress on the GIS component, *International Journal of Geographical Information Systems*, 5, pp. 373-396.

--------et al (1994) Auditory maps as alternatives to tactual maps, paper presented at the 4th International Symposium on Maps and Graphics for the Visually Impaired, São Paulo, Brazil, February 20-26.

Goodey, C.F. (1999) Politics, Nature, and Necessity: Were Aristotle's Slaves Feeble Minded?, *Political Theory*, 27(2), pp. 203-223.

Goodley, Dan (2011) *Disability Studies: An Interdisciplinary Introduction* (Los Angeles: Sage).

Goodley, Dan et al (Eds) (2012) *Disability and Social Theory: New Developments and Directions* (New York: Palgrave Macmillan)

Goodley, Dan (2011) *Disability Studies: An Interdisciplinary Introduction* (London: Sage Publications Ltd.)

Gould, C. (1988) *Information Needs in the Humanities: An Assessment* (Stanford, Calif.: Research Libraries Group).

Government of India (2005) *Disability Manual* (New Delhi: NHRC).

--------*(2006) Report of Working Group on Empowering the Disabled for Eleventh Five-Year Plan* (New Delhi: Planning Commission).

--------(undated) *Know your Rights: Rights of Persons with Disabilities* (New Delhi: NHRC).

--------(undated) *Discrimination based on Sex, Caste, Religion and Disability* (New Delhi: NHRC).

--------(n.d.) *Constitution of India, especially Part-III & IV* (New Delhi: Ministry of Law, Justice and Company Affairs).

--------(2016) Rights of Persons with Disabilities Act (New Delhi: Ministry of Law & Justice.

--------(1992) *Rehabilitation Council of India* Act (New Delhi: Ministry of Law & Justice.

--------(1999) *National Trust for Persons with Autism, Cerebral Palsy and Multiple Disabilities Act* (New Delhi: Ministry of Law & Justice.

--------(2013) *Mental Health* Act (New Delhi: Ministry of Law, & Justice.

--------(undated) *Planning a Barrier Free Environment* (New Delhi: Office of the Chief Commissioner for Persons with Disabilities).

Government of Kerala (2010) *Report of the Core Committee on Disability Studies* (Trivandrum: Department of Education).

Green, D. and Meekosha, H. (2004) *Disability Studies in Australian Universities* (Sydney: Disability Studies and Research Institute and School of Social Work, University of New South Wales).

Griffin, L.K. (1996) *Informed Consent, Sexuality, and People with Developmental Disabilities: Strategies for Professional Decision-Making* (ARC Milwaukee).

Grisham-Brown, J. et al (1998) Multi-University Collaboration via Distance Learning to Train Rural Special Education Teachers and Related Services Personnel, *Journal of Special Education Technology,* 13(4), pp. 110-121.

Grob, G.N. (1995) The Paradox of Deinstitutionalization, *Society,* July/Aug., pp. 51-59.

Groce, N. (1985) *Everyone here spoke sign language: Hereditary Deafness on Martha's Vineyard* (Cambridge, MA: Harvard University Press).

Grue, Jan (2015) *Disability and Discourse Analysis* (Surrey: Ashgate Publishing Limited).

Guffey, Elizabeth (2018) *Designing Disability: Symbols, Space, and Society* (London: Bloomsbury Academic)

Guha, S.K. (2000) Rehabilitation of the disabled: Technological support, *International Journal of Disability Studies,* special inaugural issue, Oct.- Dec., pp. 41-48.

Haggard, H. (1932) *The Lame, the Halt, and the Blind: The Vital Role of Medicine in the History of Civilization* (New York: Blue Ribbon Books).

Hagglund, Kristofer J. et al (Eds) (2006) *Handbook of Applied Disability and Rehabilitation Research* (New York: Springer Publishing Company)

Hahn, Harlan (1986) Disability and the Urban Environment: a Perspective on Los Angeles, *Environment and Planning D: Society and Space,* 4, 273-288.

--------(1985a) Disability Policy and the Problem of Discrimination, *American Behavioural Scientist,* 8, Jan.- Feb., pp. 293-318.

--------(1985b)Toward a Politics of Disability: Definitions, Disciplines, and Polices (Unpublished paper: Univ. of Southern California).

Haines, Steve and Ruebain, David (Eds)(2011) *Education, Disability and Social Policy* (Bristol: Policy Press)

Hales, G. (Ed) (1996) *Beyond Disability: Towards an Enabling Society* (Thousand Oaks, CA: Sage Publications).

Hall, Alice (2016) *Literature and Disability* (London and New York: Routledge)

Hallahan, D.P. and Koffman, J.M. (1991) *Exceptional Children: Introduction to Special Education* (London: Prentice Hall).

Hammel, J. (2006) Aids for Activities of Daily Living, In: Gary L. Albrecht et al (Eds) *Enclyclopedia of Disability*, vol. 1 (Thousand Oaks: Sage Publications).

-------- et al (2002) The Impact of Assistive Technology and Environmental Interventions on Function and Living Situation Status for People Who Are Aging with Developmental Disabilities, *Disability and Rehabilitation*, 24(1-3), pp. 93-105.

Hammel, J. and Nochajski, S. (Eds) (2001) *Aging and Developmental Disability: Current Research, Programming, and Practice Implications* (Binghamton, NY: Haworth). Holmes, M. S. (2004) *Fictions of Affliction* (Ann Arbor: Univ. of Michigan Press).

Hanes, Roy et al (Eds)(2018) *The Routledge History of Disability* (London and New York: Routledge).

Hanno-Walter Kruft (1994) *A History of Architectural Theory: From Vitruvius to the Present* (Princeton Architectural Press/PAPress).

Hans, A. et al (Eds) (2003) Women, Disability and Identity (New Delhi: Sage Publication).

Harrington, C. (2005) *Barrier- Free Travel: A Nuts and Bolts Guide for Wheelers and Slow Walkers—The Definitive Guide to Accessible Travel*, 2nd edn. (New York: Demos Medical Publishing).

--------(2005) *Barrier- Free Travel: A Nuts and Bolts Guide for Wheelers and Slow Walkers—The Definitive Guide to Accessible Travel*, 2nd edn. (New York: Demos Medical Publishing).

Harriss-White, B. (1996) *The Political Economy of Disability and Development, with Special Reference to India*, UNRISD Discussion Paper, United Nations Research Institute for Social Development (Geneva).

Hartley, S. and Muhit, M. (2003) Guest Editorial: Using qualitative research methods for disability research in majority world countries, *Asia Pacific Disability Rehabilitation Journal*, 14 (2), pp. 103-14.

Hasselbring, T.S. (2001) A possible future of special education technology, *Journal of Special Education Technology, 16*(4), pp. 15-21.

Hawes, P. and Blenkhorn, P. (2002) Bridging the Gap between Aspiration and Capability for Aphasic and Brain Injured People, *Technology and Persons with Disabilities] Conference Proceedings; available at:*http://www.csun.edu/cod/conf/2002/proceedings/220.htm.

Helal, A.S. et al (Eds) (2008) *The Engineering Handbook of Smart Technology for Aging, Disability and Independence* (New Jersey: John Wiley & Sons).

Heller, T. and Marks, B. (2006) Aging, In: Gary L. Albrecht et al (Eds) *Encyclopedia of Disability*, vol. 1 (Thousand Oaks, CA: Sage Publications), pp. 67-78.

Heron, R. and Murray, B. (2003) *Assisting Disabled Persons in Finding Employment* (Bangkok: ILO East Asia Multidisciplinary Advisory Team/ILO Regional Office for Asia and the Pacific), 2nd edn.

Herr, S. and Weber, G. (Eds) (1998) *Aging, Rights, and Quality of Life* (Baltimore: Paul H. Brookes).

Herr, S.S. et al (Eds) (2003) *The Human Rights of Persons with Intellectual Disabilities: Different but Equal* (Oxford/New York: Oxford Univ. Press).

Hillyer, B. (1993) *Feminism and Disability* (Norman, OK: University of Oklahoma Press).

Higgins, C.(2002) Physically accessible housing,*Research Information on Independent Living, 1*(9).

Higgins, E.L. and Raskind, M. H. (1997) The compensatory effectiveness of optical character recognition/speech synthesis on reading comprehension of postsecondary students with learning disabilities, *Learning Disabilities: A Multidisciplinary Journal, 8*, pp. 75-87.

Hodges, J. (Ed) (1997) *Affirmative Action in the Employment of Ethnic Minorities and Persons with Disability* (Geneva: International Labour Office).

Hoenig, H. et al (2003) Does Assistive Technology Substitute for Personal Assistance among the Disabled Elderly?, *American Journal of Public Health*, 93(2), pp. 330-337.

Hubbard, R. (1997) Abortion and disability: Who should and should not inhabit the world, In: L. Davis (Ed) *The Disability Studies Reader* (New York: Routledge), pp. 187-202.

Huebner, K.M. and Weiner, W. R. (undated) Distance Education in 2001, *Journal of Visual Impairment and Blindness*, 95(9), pp. 517-524.

Hunter-Zaworski, K (1994) *Accessing Public Transportation: New Technologies Aid Persons with Sensory or Cognitive Disabilities* (Washington, DC: Transportation Research Board).

ILO (2002) Managing disability in the workplace; available at: http://www.ilo.org/public/english/employment/skills/disability/download/code.pdf

Imrie, R.F. (1996a) *Disability and the City: International Perspectives* (London: Paul Chapman).

--------(1996b) *Disability and the City: International Perspectives* (London: Paul Chapman Publishing Ltd.).

--------(1996b) Equity, Social Justice, and Planning for Access and Disabled People: an International Perspective, *International Planning Studies*, 1 (1), pp. 17-34.

--------and Wells, P.E. (1993a) Disablism, Planning and the Built Environment, *Environment and Planning C: Government and Policy*, 11 (2), pp. 213-231

--------(1993b) Creating Barrier-Free Environments, *Town and CountryPlanning*, 61(10), pp. 278-281.

Ingstad, B. and Whyte, S. R. (Eds) (1995) *Disability and Culture* (Berkeley: University of California Press).

International Journal of Disability Studies (2010) Special issue on 'Disability Studies in Education', 4 (1 & 2), Jan.-December (New Delhi: Society for Disability and Rehabilitation Studies).

--------(2007) Special issue on 'Disability, Sexuality and Human Rights', 3 (1 & 2), Jan.- Dec., (New Delhi: Society for Disability and Rehabilitation Studies).

Irvin, C. (2004) *Home Bound: Growing up with a Disability in America* (Philadelphia: Temple University Press).

Iyer, V.R.K. (1982) *Law, Justice and the Disabled* (New Delhi: Deep & Deep).

Jaffe, M. and Smith, T.P. (1986) *Siting Homes for Developmentally Disabled Persons* (Chicago: American Planning Association).

Janicki, M. and Ansello, E. (Eds) (2000) *Community Supports for Aging Adults with Lifelong Disabilities* (Baltimore: Paul H. Brookes).

Janicki, M. P. and Dalton, A. J. (Eds) (1998) *Dementia and Aging Adults with Intellectual Disabilities: A Handbook* (Philadelphia: Francis and Taylor).

Johnston, Kirsty (2016) *Disability Theatre and Modern Drama: Recasting Moderrism* (London: Bloomsbury)

Johnstone, D. (1998) *An Introduction to Disability Studies* (London: David Fulton Publishers).

Kaminer, N. (1997) Scholars and the use of the Internet, *Library and Information Science Research*, 19, pp. 329-345.

Kanter, Arlene S. (2015) *The Development of Disability Rights Under International Law: From Charity to Human Rights* (London and New York: Routledge).

Karna, G.N. (2008) Editorial: Disability rights in a global context, *International Journal of Therapy and Rehabilitation*, 15 (10), 01 October, pp 420-421.

--------(2007a) Promotion of Disability Studies in Education, *Monograph Series No.1: Disability Studies in India: Role of Institutions of Higher Education* (New Delhi: Society for Disability and Rehabilitation Studies).

--------(2007b) Disability studies in India: new directions for future, Disability Studies in Higher Education: *Monograph Series No.* 2 (New Delhi: Society for Disability and Rehabilitation Studies).

--------(2002) Disability and human rights: an international perspective, *International Journal of Disability Studies,* special issue on 'Disability and Human Rights', 1(1), Jan.-Mar., pp. 3-27.

--------(2002b) Disability and the politics of discrimination, *Human Rights Perspective,* 1 (1), pp.

--------(2001) *Disability Studies in India: Retrospects and Prospects* (New Delhi: Gyan Publishing House).

--------(2000a) Impaired rehabilitation, *The Pioneer* (New Delhi), Jan. 24.

--------(2000b) Disability Studies in India: issues and challenges, *International Journal of Disability Studies,* inaugural issue on 'Disability and Social Policy in the New Millennium',1(1), Oct.-Dec., pp. 20-40.

--------(2000c) Disability rights movement: conceptual framework and its implications for India, *Disabilities and Impairments,* 14(1), 15-22.

-------- (1999a) *United Nations and Rights of Disabled Persons: A Study in Indian Perspective* (New Delhi: APH Publishing Corporation).

-------- (1999b) Disabled perspective, *The Pioneer* (New Delhi), Dec.8.

--------and Gaharana, K. (1994) Disability and the rights of disabled persons, In: K. P. Saksena (Ed) *Human Rights : Perspective and Challenges beyond 1990s* (New Delhi: Lancer Books).

Kasnitz, D. and Shuttleworth, R. P. (Eds) (2001, Summer) Theme: Engaging Anthropology in Disability Studies, *Disability Studies* Quarterly, 21 (3).

Kaufman, M. et al (2003) *Ultimate Guide to Sex and Disability* (California: CLEIS).

Keith, L. (Ed) (1994) *Mustn't grumble: Writings by Disabled Women* (London: The Women's Press).

Kemp, B.J. and Mosqueda, L. (2004) *Aging with a Disability: What the Clinician Needs to Know* (Baltimore: Johns Hopkins University Press).

Kempton, W. (1998) *Socialization and Sexuality: A Comprehensive Training Guide for Professionals Helping People with Disabilities That Hinder Learning (Program Development Associates).*

Kennedy, J. (Ed) (2003) Journal of Disability Policy Studies, Special Issue on Disability and Aging, 12(4).

Kerschbaum, Stephanie L et al (Eds) (2017) Negotiating Disability: Disclosure and Higher *Education* (Ann Arbor: University of Michigan Press)

Kessel, Martina and Merziger, Patrick (Eds)(2012) *The Politics of Humour: Laughter, Inclusion, and Exclusion in the Twentieth Century* (University of Toronto Press)

King, R. et al (2007) *Handbook of Psychosocial Rehabilitation* (Blackwell Publishing).

Kirk, S. A. et al (2006) *Educating Exceptional Children* (Houghton Miffin, USA).

Kittay, E. et al (Eds)(2001) Special issue: Feminism and Disability, *Hypatia*, 16(4).

Klatzky, R.L. et al (1990) Acquisition of route and survey knowledge in the absence of vision, *Journal of Motor Behavior*, 22, 1, pp. 19-43.

Kluth, P. et al (Eds) (n.d.) *Access to Academics for All Students: Critical Approaches to Inclusive Curriculum, Instruction, and Policy* (New Jersey: Lawrence Erlbaum Associates, Publishers).

Kogut, J. and Vilardo, Susan (1993) *Teaching Persons with Mental Retardation about Sexuality and Relationships: An Instructional Guide* (Planned Parenthood of Connecticut).

Kose, S. (1998) From barrier-free to universal design: An international perspective, *Assistive Technology, 10*(1), pp. 44-50.

Kridler, C. and Stewart, R.K. (1992a) Access for the Disabled 1, *Progressive Architecture*, 73 (7), pp. 41-42.

--------(1992b) Access for the Disabled 2, *Progressive Architecture*, 73 (8), pp. 35-36.

--------(1992c) Access for the Disabled 3, *Progressive Architecture*, 73 (9), pp. 45-46.

Krieger, L.H. (2003). *Backlash against the ADA: Reinterpreting Disability Rights (*Ann Arbor, MI: University of Michigan Press).

Kristiansen, K. (2008) *Arguing about Disability: Philosophical Perspectives* (London: Routledge).

Kroll, Thilo (Ed) (2007) *Focus on Disability: Trends in Research and Application,* Vol. II (New York: Nova Biomedical Books)

Kumari, Sandhya (2018a) 'A Sociological Study of Disabled Characters as Depicted in Hindi Prose' (in Hindi), PhD Thesis submitted to Jawaharlal Nehru University, New Delhi, India (unpublished).

--------(Ed) (2018b) *A Collection of Disabled Character-based Hindi Stories-in Hindi* (unpublished).

Kuppers, P. (2003) *Disability and Contemporary Performance: Bodies on Edge* (London and New York: Routledge).

Lebovich, W.L. (1993) *Design for Dignity: Studies in Accessibility* (New York: Wiley).

Lahm, E. and Morrissette, S. (1994) Zap 'em with assistive technology, Paper presented at the annual meeting of The Council for Exceptional Children, Denver, CO, April.

Lance, G.D. (2002) Distance Learning and Disability: A View From the Instructor's Side of the Virtual Lectern, *Information Technology and Disabilities,* (8)(1), Special Issue: Distance Education and Disability, January.

Langston, C. (2001) *Sustainable Practices in the Built Environment* (Butterworth Heinemann).

LaPlante, M. P. et al (1997) The Prevalence of Need for Assistive Technology Devices and Home Accessibility Features, *Technology & Disability,* 6(1/2), pp. 17-28.

Lazar, Jonathan and Stein, Michael Ashley (Eds) (2017) *Disability, Human Rights, and Information Technology* (Philadelphia: University of Pennsylvania Press)

Lazinger, S.S. et al (1997) Internet use by faculty members in various disciplines: A comparative case study, *Journal of the American Society for Information Science,* 48(6), pp. 508-518.

Lee, C. (1999) *Learning Disabilities and Assistive Technologies: An Emerging Way to Touch the Future* (Amherst, MA: McGowan Publications).

Lerner, N. and Straus, J. N. (Eds) (2006) *Sounding Off: Theorizing Disability in Music* (New York: Routledge).

Lesnik-Oberstein, Karín (Eds)(2015) *Rethinking Disability Theory and Practice: Challenging Essentialism* (Houndmills: Palgrave Macmillan)

Lifchez, R. and Winslow, B. (1979) *Design for Independent Living: the Environment and Physically Disabled People* (London: Architectural Press).

Linett, Maren Tova (2017) *Bodies of Modernism: Physical Disability in Transatlantic Modernist Literature* (Ann Arbor: University of Michigan Press)

Linton, S. (2007) *Body Politic: A Memoir* (Ann Arbor: Univ. of Michigan Press).

--------(1998) *Claiming Disability: Knowledge and Identity* (New York: New York University Press).

Liu, L. et al (2001) Evaluation of technologies for distance delivery of continuing education to rehabilitation professionals, *The AT Odyssey Continues: Proceedings of the RESNA 2001 Annual Conference,* June 22-26 (Reno, NV, RESNA Press, Arlington, VA), pp. 163-165.

Longmore, P. K. (2003) *Why I Burned My Book and Other Essays on Disability* (Philadelphia: Temple University Press).

--------and Umansky, L. (Eds.) (2001) *The New Disability History: American Perspectives* (New York University Press).

Lönnqvist, H. (1990) Scholars seek information: Information-seeking behaviour and information needs of humanities scholars, *International Journal of Information and Library Research,* 2(3), pp. 195-203.

Lonsdale, S. (1990) *Women and Disability* (New York: St. Martin's Press).

Loomis, J.M. et al (1993) *Personal guidance system for the visually impaired using GPS, GIS, and VR technologies,* paper presented at the Conference on Virtual Reality and Persons with Disabilities, San Francisco, California, June 17-18.

Ludlow, B.L. and Brannan, S.A. (1999) Distance Education Program Preparing Personnel for Rural Areas: Current Practices, Emerging Trends, and Future Directions, *Rural Special Education Quarterly*, 18 (3-4), pp. 5-20.

Lueck, A. H. (undated) Live and Online: A Year-round Training Program for Teachers of Students with Visual Impairments in California, *Journal of Visual Impairment and Blindness*, 95(9), pp. 533-542.

MacArthur, C.A. (1996) Using technology to enhance the writing processes of students with learning disabilities, *Journal of Learning Disabilities, 29*(4), pp. 344-354.

Mace, R.L. (1998) Universal design in housing, *Assistive Technology,10*(1), pp. 21-28.

Mackelprang, R.W. and Valentine, D. (Eds) (1996) *Sexuality and Disabilities: A Guide for Human Service Practitioners* (The Haworth Press, Inc.).

Mackelprang, R.W. and Salsgiver, R. O. (1998) *Disability: A Diversity Model Approach in Human Service Practice* (Washington, Lyceum).

Maisel, J.L. (2006) Toward inclusive housing and neighborhood design: a look at visitability, *Community Development: Journal of the Community Development Society, 37*(3), pp. 26-34.

Male, M. (1994) *Technology for Inclusion: Meeting the Special Needs of All Students* (Boston: Allyn and Bacon).

Manduchi, Roberto and Sri Kurniawan (2012) *Assistive Technology for Blindness and Low Vision* (Boca Raton: CRC Press)

Manjula, R. (2004) Overview and Current Status of Augmentative and Alternative Communication, In: M. Jayaram and R. Manjula (Eds) *Augmentative & Alternative Communication*, Proceedings of the Continuing Education

Program on Augmentative and Alternative Communication (Mysore: All India Institute of Speech and Hearing).

Mann, W.C. et al (1999) Effectiveness of Assistive Technology and Environmental Interventions in Maintaining Independence and Reducing Home Care Costs for the Frail Elderly: A Randomized Controlled Trial, *Archives of Family Medicine,* 8, pp. 210-217.

Marks, D. (1999) *Disability: Controversial Debates and Psychosocial Perspectives* (New York: Routledge).

Marshall, J.G. (1990) Diffusion of innovation theory and end-user searching, *Library and Information Science Research,* 12, pp. 55-69.

Mason, J. (2002) *Qualitative Researching* (London: Sage Publications), 2nd edn.

McConkey, R. (2005) Service delivery in low- income countries, In: E. Alant and L.L. Lloyd (Eds) *Augmentative and Alternative Communication and Severe Disabilities: Beyond Poverty* (London, UK: Whurr), pp. 131-154.

McLeod, J.(2009) *An Introduction to Counselling,* 4th edn. (Maidenhead: Open University Press).

Mercer, C.D. (1997) *Students with Learning Disabilities* (New Jersey: Merril Prentice Hall).

Miles, M.B., and Huberman, M.(1984) *Qualitative Data Analysis: A Sourcebook of New Methods* (Beverly Hills: Sage Publications).

Minow, M. (1990) *Making all the Difference: Inclusion, Exclusion, and American Law* (Ithaca, NY: Cornell University Press).

Mintz, S. (2007) *Unruly Bodies: Life Writings by Women with Disabilities* (Chapel Hill: University of North Carolina).

Mitchell, D.T. and Snyder, S. L. (2003) *Narrative Prosthesis: Disability and the Dependencies of Discourse* (Ann Arbor: University of Michigan Press).

Mitra, S. (2006) The capability approach and disability, *Journal of Disability Policy Studies,* 16 (4), pp. 236-247.

Morris, J. (1991) *Pride against Prejudice: A Personal Politics of Disability* (London: The Women's Press).

--------(1989) *Abled Lives: Women's Experiences of Paralysis* (London: The Women's Press).

Morton, H.C., and Price, A.J. (1989) *ACLS Survey of Scholars: A Final Report of Views on Publications, Computers, and Libraries* (Washington, D.C.: American Council of Learned Societies).

Mautone, O. (undated) The Cost Benefit Analysis and the Environment in Community Structural Funds in Italy, available at: http://www.crrconference.org/downloads/mautone1.pdf

McKeown, S. (2000 *Unlocking Potential - How ICT can support children with special needs* (The Questions Publishing Company Ltd.).

McLeod, J. (2009) *An Introduction to Counselling*, 4th edn. (Maidenhead: Open University Press).

McNear, D. (2003) A Framework for Braille Literacy: Integrative Assistive Technology in the Literacy Curriculum, Assistive Technology Application & Integration Nova Scotia ATAINS Assistive Technology 'Best Practices' Conference April 3-5.

McNeese, Tim (2014) *Disability Rights Movement* (Minneapolis: ABDO Publishing Company).

Meekosha, H. (2005) *Body Battles: Disability, Representation,and Participation* (Thousand Oaks, CA: Sage).

--------(2000)*Narrative Prosthesis: Disability and the Dependencies of Discourse* (Ann Arbor: University of Michigan Press).

Menendez, F. (2006) Access through architecture: Accessible classroom, *PN/Paraplegia News, 60*(10), pp. 20-26.

Metzler, Irina (2013) *Disability in Medieval Europe: Thinking about Physical Impairment during the high Middle Ages,* c. 1100-1400 (London: Routledge).

Milner, J. and O'Byrne, P. (2002) *Brief Counselling: Narratives and Solutions* (Basingstoke: Palgrave).

Mishra, A.K. and R. Gupta (2006) Measurement of Disability-Disability Index: A Measure of Deprivation among Disabled, *Economic and Political Weekly*, 41 (38), pp. 4026-4029.

Mitchell, D. and Snyder, S. (2001) Representation and its Discontents: The Uneasy Home of Disability in Literature and Film, In: Gary L. Albrecht et al (Eds) *Handbook of Disability Studies (Thousand Oaks,CA: Sage).*

--------(Eds)(1997) *The Body and Physical Difference: Discourses of Disability* (Ann Arbor: University of Michigan Press).

Mitra, S. and U. Sambamoorthi (2008) Disability and the Rural Labor Market in India: Evidence for Males in Tamil Nadu, *Economic and Political Weekly*, 36 (5), pp. 934-952.

--------(2006a) Measurement of Disability— Disability Estimates in India: What the Census and NSS Tell Us, *Economic and Political Weekly*, 41(38), pp. 4022-4025.

--------(2006b)Perspectives-Employment of Persons with Disabilities: Evidence from the National Sample Survey, *Economic and Political Weekly*, 41 (3), pp. 199-203.

Monro, S. (2005) *Gender Politics* (London: Pluto Press).

Moore, G.C., and Benbasat, I. (1991) Development of an instrument to measure the perceptions of adopting an information technology innovation, *Information Systems Research*, 2(3), 1991, pp. 192-222.

Moore, R. (2000) For Knowledge: Traditions Progressivison and Progress in Education Restructuring the Curriculum Debate, *Cambridge Journal of Education*, 30(1), pp. 17-36.

Morasso, P. et al (1979) *Towards Standardization of Communication and Control Systems for Motor Impaired People* (Berlin; Springer),17 (4), pp.

Morris, R.J. (Ed) (2008) *Disability Research and Policy: Current Perspectives* (New Jersey: Lawrence Erlbaum Associates Publishers).

Morris, J. (1998) *Pride against prejudice: Transforming Attitudes to Disabilities*, rep. (North Pomfret, VT: Trafalgar Square).

--------(1993) Feminism and disability, *Feminist Review*, 43, pp. 57-70.

--------(1992) Personal and political: A feminist perspective on researching physical disability, *Disability, Handicap & Society*, 7 (2), pp. 157-166.

Mossman, Mark (2009) *Disability, Representation and the Body in Irish Writing: 1800-1922* (Houndmills: Palgrave Macmillan)

Muecke, M. (1997) Policy as forethought in qualitative research. A paradigm from developing country social scientists, In: J. Morse (Ed) *Completing a qualitative project* (London, Sage publications).

Murickan, J. and Kareparamil, G. (1995) *Persons with Disabilities in Society* (Trivandrum: Kerala Federation of the Blind).

Nas, T.F. (1996) *Cost-Benefit Analysis: Theory and Application* (Thousand Oaks, California: Sage).

Neistadt, M.E. and Freda, M. (1987) *Choices: A Guide to Sex Counseling with Physically Disabled Adults,* illustrated by Kerry Anne O'Reilly (Krieger Publishing Company).

Nicolle, C. and Abascal, J. (Eds) *Inclusive Design Guidelines for HCI* (London and New York: Taylor & Francis).

Nisbet, P. and Poon, P. (1998) *Special Access Technology* (University of Edinburgh: The CALL Centre).

-------- et al (1999) *Supportive Writing Technology* (University of Edinburgh: The CALL Centre).

Nitnaware, R.C. (2006) *Home Instructions on Physiotherapy in the field of Mental Retardation* (Secunderabad: NIMH).

Nizar, Smitha (2016) *The Contradiction in Disability Law: Selective Abortions and Rights* (New Delhi: OUP).

Norwich, B. (2008) *Dilemmas of Difference, Inclusion and Disability: International Perspectives and Future Directions* (Oxon: Routledge).

Nussbaum, M.C. (2006) *Frontiers of Justice: Disability, Nationality Species Membership* (Oxford University Press).

O' Brien, R. (Ed) (2004) *Voices from the Edge* (Oxford University Press).

--------(2001) *Crippled Justice: The History of Modern Disability Policy in the Workplace* (Chicago: University of Chicago Press).

O'Day, B.L. and Corcoran, P. J. (1994) Assistive Technology: Problems and Policy Alternatives, *Archives of Physical Medicine and Rehabilitation*, 75, pp. 1165-1169.

Ogden, D. (1997) *The Crooked Kings of Ancient Greece* (London: Duckworth).

Okolo, C.M. (2005) Interactive technologies and social studies instruction for students with mild disabilities, In: D. Edyburn et al (Eds) *The Handbook of Special Education Technology Research and Practice* (Milwaukee, WI: Knowledge by Design), pp. 623-641.

Oliver, M. (1996) *Understanding Disability: From Theory to Practice* (Houndmills, Macmillan Pvt. Limited).

--------and N. Watson (2001) The social model of disability: an outdated ideology?, *Research in Social Science and Disability*, 2, pp 9-28.

Oliver, M. (1990) *The Politics of Disablement* (London: The MacMillan Press).

Olkin, Rhoda and Pledger, Constance (2003) Can Disability Studies and Psychology join Hands, *American Psychologist*, 58 94), pp. 256-304.

Olsen, R. and Clarke, H. (2003) *Parenting and Disability: Disabled Parents' Experiences of Raising Children* (Bristol: The Polity Press).

Olson, R.K. and Wise, B.W. (1992) Reading on the computer with orthographic and speech feedback. *Reading and Writing: An Interdisciplinary Journal, 4, pp.* 107-144.

Olyan, S.M. (2008) *Disability in the Hebrew Bible: Interpreting Mental and Physical Differences* (Cambridge University Press).

Orpwood, R. (1990) Design methodology for aids for the disabled, Journal of *Medical Engineering Technology*, Jan-Feb; 14(1), pp. 2-10.

Orr, R.J. (2003) *My Right to Play: A Child with Complex Needs* (Maidenhead: Open University Press).

O'Sullivan, E. and Rassel, G.R. (1995) *Research Methods for Public Administrators* (White Plains, NY: Longman).

Osgood, R.L. (2008) *The History of Special Education: A Struggle for Equality in American Public Schools* (London: Praeger).

Pace, R.J. and Young, L. (2002) Future housing now: The next generation universal home, In: *R. Simpson (Ed) Proceedings of the RESNA 25th International Conference: Technology and Disability: Research, Design, Practice and Policy* (Arlington, VA: RESNA Press).

Pain, H. et al (2003) *Choosing Assistive Devices: A Guide for Users and Professionals* (London: Jessica Kingsley Publishers).

Pandey, S. and Chirimar, Priyanka (2005) *Disability and the Law* (New Delhi: Human Rights Network).

Pandit, I. (1992) *Informal Communication in the Humanities: A Qualitative Inquiry*, unpublished doctoral dissertation (Urbana-Champaign: University of Illinois at Urbana-Champaign).

Pao, M.L. (1982) Collaboration in computational musicology, *Journal of the American Society for Information Science*, 33(1), pp. 38-43.

Peek, R.P. (1997) 'Early Use of Worldwide Electronic Mailing Lists by Social Science and Humanities Scholars in the United States', unpublished doctoral dissertation (New York: Syracuse University).

Panek, P. et al (2001) Smart Home Applications for disabled Persons - Experiences and Perspectives; Reprint from "EIB Event 2001 - Proceedings"; (2001), S. 71-80; available at: http://publik.tuwien.ac.at/files/pub-et_4384.pdf

Parker, G. (1993) *With this Body: Caring and Disability in Marriage* (Buckingham: University Press).

Pearman, Tory Vandeventer (2010) *Women and Disability in Medieval Literature* (New York: Palgrave Macmillan)

Peate, I. and Fearns, D. (Eds) (2006) *Caring for People with Learning Disabilities* (West Sussex: John Wiley & Sons).

Perkins, M. (2007) *Pragmatic Impairment* (Cambridge University Press).

Perlin, Michael L. and Lynch, Alison J. (2016) *Sexuality, Disability, and the Law: Beyond the Last Frontier?* (Houndmills: Palgrave Macmillan)

Peterson, W. (1998) Public policy affecting universal design, *Assistive Technology, 10*(1), 13-20.

Pfeiffer, D. (1990) Public Transit Access for Disabled Persons in the United States, *Disability & Society*, 5 (2), pp. 153-66.

Philips, B. and Zhao, H. (1993) Predictors of Assistive Technology Abandonment, *Assistive Technology*, 5, pp. 36-45.

Pisha, B. and Coyne, P. (2001) Smart from the Start: The Promise of Universal Design for Learning, *Remedial and Special Education*, 22(4), July/August, pp. 197-203.

Prasher, V. P. and Janicki, M. P. (Eds) (2002) *Physical Health of Adults with Intellectual Disabilities* (Oxford: Blackwell Publishing Limited).

Potter, J. and Wetherell, M. (1987) Discourse and Social Psychology (London: Sage).

Shakespeare, T. (1996) Disability, Identity and Difference, In: Colin Barnes and Geof Mercer (Eds) *Exploring the Divide* (Leeds: The Disability Press), pp. 94-113.

Poulson, D. et al (Eds) (1996) *Userfit: A Practical Handbook on User-centred Design for Assistive Technology* (TIDE USER consortium).

Prasher, V. P. (Ed) (2010) *Contemporary Issues in Intellectual Disabilities: Disability Studies* (New York: Nova Science Publishers, Inc.)

Priestley, M. (2003) *Disability: A Life Course Approach* (Cambridge: Polity Press).

--------(1999) *Disability Politics and Community Care* (London:Jessica Kingsley Publishers).

Proudman, A. (2007) Brief Reports towards the Development of Augmentative and Alternative Communication Practice in a Special Needs Setting in Bangalore, India, *Asia Pacific Disability Rehabilitation Journal*, 18 (2), pp. 131-145.

Pullin, Graham (2009) *Design Meets Disability* (Cambridge: MIT Press)

Punch, K.F. (1998) *Introduction to Social Research: Quantitative and Qualitative Approaches* (London: Sage).

Putisek, M. et al (1999) New Opportunities: Distance Learning for People with Special Needs, *Assistive Technology on the Threshold of the New Millennium, AAATE* [Association for the Advancement of Assistive Technology in Europe] *1999 Conference Proceedings*, Amsterdam, pp. 86-89.

Quinn, G. and Degener, T. (2002) *Human Rights and Disability* (New York: United Nations).

Quinn, P. (1998) *Understanding Disability: A Lifespan Approach* (Thousand Oaks: California; Sage Publications).

Raj, S.L.(1998) *Fifty Years after Freedom* (New Delhi: Indian Social Institute).

Rajalakshmi, K. (2002) Social Issues: A Law on Paper,*The Frontline*,19 (7), Mar. 30-April 12.

Rao, L. Govinda et al (2005) *Status of Education of Children with Disabilities* (Secunderabad: NIMH).

Ravneberg, Bodil and Soderstrom, Sylvia (2017) *Disability, Society and Assistive Technology* (London and New York: Routledge).

Ray, Sarah Jaquette and Sibara, Jay (Eds) (2017) *Disability Studies and the Environmental Humanities : Toward an Eco-Crip Theory* (University of Nebraska)

Reddy, G.L. and Poornima, R. (2007) Disability and sexuality:a special education perspectives, *International Journal of Disability Studies*, 3 (1 & 2).

--------(2008)Disability and sexuality: teaching and research perspectives, *International Journal of Disability Studies*, 4 (1 & 2).

Reddy, G. L. and Poornima, R. (2009) Integration of Disability Studies in general curriculum at school and college levels in India: a critical appraisal, *University News*, 47 (17).

Reddy, G. L. (2009) Promoting inclusive schools: issues and practices, *International Educator*, 20 (1).

--------(2009) Education, research and innovations for inclusive societies, in: Souvenir of the International Conference, held at School of Education & HRD, Dravidian University, Kuppam (AP), March.

--------(2007) Inclusive education: supportive systems for students with disabilities in higher education, *University News*, 45 (14).

--------(2007) *Occupational Stress, Professional Burn out and Job Satisfaction of Special Education Teachers* (New Delhi: Discovery Publishing House).

--------(2006) Students with specific learning difficulties: detection and management, *Edutracks*, 6 (1), September.

--------(2006) *Children with Disabilities: Awareness, Attitude and Competencies of Teachers* (New Delhi: Discovery Publishing House).

--------(2005) Special Education in Western Countries and India: A Comparative Study, *International Journal of Disability Studies*, 1 (1), pp.

--------*et al (2005) Anti- Social Behaviour in Children: Detection and Management* (New Delhi: Discovery Publishing House).

--------et al (2005) *Behaviour Disorders in Children: Identification, Assessment and Intervention Strategies* (New Delhi: Discovery Publishing House).

--------et al(2005) *Behaviour Disorder in Students: Detection and Management* (New Delhi: Discovery Publishing House).

--------et al (2004) *Mental Retardation: Education and Rehabilitation Services* (New Delhi: Discovery Publishing House).

--------et al (2004) *Hearing Impairment: An Educational Consideration* (New Delhi: Discovery Publishing House).

--------et al (2003) *Education of Children with Special Needs* (New Delhi: Discovery Publishing House).

--------et al (1999) Assistive technology to overcome learning difficulties in children, *Journal of Disabilities and Impairments*, 13 (1 & 2).

--------et al (2004) *Mental Retardation: Education and Rehabilitation Services* (New Delhi: Discovery Publishing House).

--------et al (2000) *Learning Disabilities: A Practical Guide to Practitioners* (New Delhi: Discovery Publishing House).

Reinders, H. (2000) *The Future of the Disabled in Liberal Society: An Ethical Analysis* (Notre Dame: University of Notre Dame Press).

Reinkensmeyer, D.J. et al (2004) Robotics, Motor Learning, and Neurologic Recovery, *Annual Review of Biomedical Engineering*, 6, pp. 497–525.

Riddell, S. (1999) *Disability and Civil Rights in the New Millennium* (University of Glasgow: Strathclyde Centre for Disability Research).

Riddle, Christpher A. (2017) *Human Rights, Disability, and Capabilities* (New York: Springer)

Rifkin, S. and Hartley, S. (1999) *Teaching qualitative methods for disability research*, Saudi Journal of Disability and Rehabilitation, 5 (1), pp. 7-15.

Rimmer, J. H. et al (2004) Improvements in Physical Fitness in Adults with Down Syndrome, *American Journal on Mental Retardation*,109(2), pp.165-174.

Rimmerman, Arie (2015) *Family Policy and Disability* (Cambridge University Press)

Rioux, Marcia H. et al (Eds) (2011) *Critical Perspectives on Human Rights and Disability Law* (Leiden and Boston: Martinus Nijhoff Publishers)

Rioux, M.H. (1997) When Myths Masquerade as Science: Disability Research from an Equality-Rights Perspective, In: Len Barton and Mike Oliver (Eds) *Disability Studies: Past, Present and Future* (Leeds: The Disability Press).

--------and Bach, M. (Eds) (1994) *Disability is not Measles: New Research Paradigms in Disability* (North York, Ont.: The Roeher Institute).

Rispler-Chaim (2007) *Disability in Islamic Law* (The Netherlands: Springer).

Rogers, E.M. (1995) *Diffusion of Innovations*, 4th ed. (New York: The Free Press).

Rogers, J. (2006) *The Disabled Women's Guide to Pregnancy and Birth* (New York: Demos Medical Publishers).

Romski, M. and Sevcik, R. (2005) *Augmentative Communication and Early Intervention: Myths and Realities*. Infants and Young Children, 18 (3), pp. 174-185.

Rose, D. and Meyer, A. (2000) Universal design for individual differences, *Educational Leadership*, 58(3), pp. 39-43.

Rose, M. (2003) *The Staff of Oedipus:Transforming Disability in Ancient Greece* (Ann Arbor: University of Michigan Press).

Rosen, M. J. (Ed) (2002) Recollections and Perspectives, special issue of the *Journal of Rehabilitation Research and Development*, 39(6); available at: www.vard.org/jour/02/39/6/sup/contents.html

Rosenbaum, H. and Snyder, H. (1991) An investigation of emerging norms in computer mediated communication: An empirical study of computer conferencing, *Proceedings of the ASIS Annual Meeting*, Washington, DC: 28, pp. 15-23.

Ruth, S. R., and Gouet, R. (1993) Must invisible colleges be invisible? An approach to examining large communities of network users, *Internet Research*, 3(1), pp. 36-51.

Ro Rothstein, L. (1991) Campuses and the Disabled, *The Chronicle of Higher Education*, September 4, pp. B4, B10.

Roulstone, Alan and Prideaux, Simon (2012) Understanding Disability Policy (Bristol: Policy Press), also available at: file: ///C:/ Users /sfd/ Downloads/Alan% 20Roulstone%20and%20Simon%20Pr ideaux-Understanding%20Disability%20Policy-Policy%20Press%20(2012)%20(1).pdf

Rungta, S.K. (2004) Training and Employment of People with Disabilities: India 2002 (ILO), *GLADNET Collection*, Cornell University ILR School Year, also available at: http://digitalcommons.ilr.cornell.edu/cgi/viewcontent.cgi?article=1470&co ntext=gladnetcollect

Safford, P.L. and Safford, E. J. (1996) *A History of Childhood & Disability* (New York: Teachers College Press).

Sandowski, Carol L. (1989) *Sexual Concerns When Illness or Disability Strikes* (Charles C. Thomas Publisher, Ltd.).

Sargent, C.A. et al (2001) The Ohio Assistive Technology Distance Learning Project: Evolution to Web-based Education and the Implementation of an Impact Study, *The AT Odyssey Continues: Proceedings of the RESNA 2001 Annual Conference*, June 22-26 (Reno, NV, RESNA Press, Arlington, VA), pp. 208-210.

Sax, C. (1999) Distance Education: Taking It to the Next Level, *Spotlight on Technology, Proceedings of the RESNA 1999 Annual Conference*, June 25-29 (Long Beach, CA, RESNA Press, Arlington, VA), pp. 291-293.

--------(1998) Learning from a Distance: Assistive Technology Training for Rehabilitation Counselors, *The State of the Arts and Science, Proceedings of the RESNA 1998 Annual Conference*, Minneapolis, MN, June 26-30 (RESNA Press, Arlington, VA), pp. 311-313.

Saxton, M. and Howe, F. (Eds) (1993) *With Wings: An Anthology of Literature by and about Women with Disabilities* (New York: Feminist Press at the City University of New York).

Scadden, L.A. (1998) The Internet and the Education of Students with Disabilities, *Technology and Disability*, 8(3), pp. 141-148.

Schaefermeyer, M. T., and Sewell, E. H. (1988) Communicating by electronic mail, *American Behavioral Scientist*, 32, pp. 112-123.

Schenker, K.T. and Scadden, L.A. (2002) The Design of Accessible Distance Education Environments that Use Collaborative Learning, *Information Technology and Disabilities*, (8)(1), Special Issue: Distance Education and Disability, January.

Scherer, M.J. (2005) *Living in the State of Stuck: How Assistive Technology Impacts the Lives of People with Disabilities,* 4th Edition (Cambridge, MA: Brookline Books).

--------(2004) *Connecting to Learn: Educational and Assistive Technology for People with Disabilities*. (Washington, DC: American Psychological Association (APA Books).

--------(Ed)(2002) *Assistive Technology: Matching Device and Consumer for Successful Rehabilitation* (Washington, DC: APA Books).

Schlesinger, L. and Taub, D.E. (Eds)(2003) I*nstructional Materials for Sociology and Disability Studies* (Washington, DC: ASA Teaching Resources Center).

Schnorr, J.M. (1999) Developing and Using Technology for Course Delivery, *Teacher and Special Education*, 22(2), pp. 114-122.

Scotch, R. (2001) *From Good Will to Civil Rights: Transforming Federal Disability Policy* (Philadelphia: Temple University Press).

Shapiro, J.P. (1993) *No Pity: People with Disabilities Forging a New Civil Rights Movement* (New York: Times Books).

Schover, L.R. (1988) *Sexuality and Chronic Illness: A Comprehensive Approach* (Guilford Publications).

Seale, J.K. (2006) *E-Learning and Disability in Higher Education: Accessibility Research and Practice* (London and New York: Routledge).

Sen, Amartya (n. d.) Disability and justice, retrieved at: http://72.14.235.132/search?q =cache:gNVnh8e09Ng J:siteresources.worldbank.org/DISABILITY/214576-1092421729901/20291152/Amartya_Sen _Speech. doc+ Amartya +Sen+ disability&hl =en&ct=clnk &cd=1&gl= in

Sen, Amartya and J. D. Wolfensohn (2004) Helping disabled people out of the shadows, *The Korea Times,* 21 December, retrieved at: http://tinyurl.com/4vbzhw (accessed 15 September 2008).

Sen, Anima (1992) *Mental Handicap among Rural Indian Children (New Delhi:* Sage Publications).

Shah, S. (2007) *Sustainable Practice for the Facilities Manager* (Wiley- Blackwell).

Shakespeare, T. (Ed) (2015) *Disability Research Today: International Perspectives* (London and New York: Routledge)

--------et al (2001) *Making the Difference: disability, politics,* recognition, in: Gary A. Albrecht et al (Eds) *Handbook of Disability Studies (*Thousand Oaks: Sage), pp. 546-564.

--------(Ed) (1998) *The Disability Reader: Social Science Perspectives* (London: Cassell).

--------(1996a) *Disability, Identity and Difference,* in: Colin Barnes and Geof Mercer (Eds) *Exploring the Divide: Illness and Disability* (Leeds: The Disability Press).

--------et al (Eds) (1996b) *The Sexual Politics of Disability: Untold Desires* (Leeds: The Disability Press).

Sheila, A.M. M. and Williamson, L. (2007) *Impairment and Disability: Law and Ethics at the Beginning and End of Life* (New York: Routledge- Cavendish).

Shildrick, Margrit (2009) *Dangerous Discourses of Disability, Subjectivity and Sexuality* Houndmills: Palgrave Macmillan)

Siegel-Causey, E. and Guess, D. (1989) *Enhancing Nonsymbolic Communication Interactions among Learners with Severe Disabilities* (Baltimore: Paul H. Brookes).

Silvers, A. et al (1998) *Disability Difference Discrimination: Perspectives on Justice in Bioethics and Public Policy* (Lanham: Rowman & Littlefield Publishers).

Stephen, T. and Harrison, T.M. (1994) Comserve, moving the communication discipline online, *Journal of the American Society for Information Science,* 45(10), pp. 765-770.

Stein, M. S. (2006) *Distributive Justice Disability Utilitarianism against Egalitarianism* (New Haven and London: Yale University Press).

Strauss, A., and Corbin, J. (1990) *Basics of Qualitative Research: Grounded Theory Procedures and Techniques* (Newbury Park, CA: Sage).

Swain, J. et al (Eds) (1993) *Disabling Barriers Enabling Environments* (New Delhi: Sage Publications).

Sharma, Umesh (2005) Integrated Education in India: Challenges and Prospects, *Disability Studies Quarterly*, 25 (1), available at: www.dsq-sds.org

Singhal, Nidhi (2008) *Forgotten Youth: Disability and Development in India* (Cambridge: Research Consortium on Educational Outcomes and Poverty), retrieved at: http://recoup.educ.cam.ac.uk/publications/WP14-NS.pdf

Shah, S. (2010) Role of family in empowering the young disabled people, *International Journal of Disability Studies*, special issue on 'Disability Studies in Education: emerging issues', 4 (1 & 2), Jan.- Dec.

Shakespeare, Tom (Ed) (2015) *Disability Research Today: International Perspectives* (London and New York: Routledge)

--------.(Ed)(1998) *The Disability Reader: Social Science Perspectives* (London/New York: Cassell).

--------(2006) *Disability Rights and Wrongs* (Oxon: Routledge).

--------(1996) *Rules of engagement: doing disability research, Disability and Society*, 11 (1), pp. 115-119.

--------(1994) Cultural representation of disabled people: dustbins for disavowal?, *Disability & Society*, 9, pp. 283-299.

Shapiro, A. (1999) *Everybody Belongs: Changing Negative Attitudes toward Classmates with Disabilities* (New York: Routledge Falmer).

Shapiro, J. P. (1994) *No Pity* (New Delhi: Universal Law Publishing).

Stainton, T. (2003) Reason's other: the emergence of the disabled subject in the Northern Renaissance, *Disability & Society*, 9, pp. 225-243.

Schillmeier, Michael (2010) *Rethinking Disability: Bodies, Senses, and Things* (New York: Routledge)

Sheila, A.M.M. and Williamson, L. (2007) *Impairment and Disability: Law and Ethics at the Beginning and End of Life* (New York: Routledge- Cavendish).

Sie, I.H. et al (1992) Upper extremity pain in the postrehabilitation spinal cord injured patient, *Archives of Physical Medicine and Rehabilitation*, 73, pp. 44-48

Siebers, Tobin (2008) *Disability Theory—Corporealities: Discourses of Disability* (Ann Arbor: University of Michigan Press)

Sipski, M.L. and Alexander, C. J. (1997) *Sexual Function in People With Disability and Chronic Illness: A Health Professional's Guide* (Aspen Publishers Inc.).

Siraisi, N.G. (1990) *Medieval & Early Renaissance Medicine: An Introduction to Knowledge and Practice* (Chicago: University of Chicago Press).

Skinner, P. (1997) *Health and Medicine in Early Medieval Southern Italy* (Leiden, the Netherlands, and New York: E. J. Brill).

Smith, Julia L.T. (2015) *Women, Disability and Mental Distress* (Surrey: Ashgate Publishing Limited)

Skrtic, T.M. (Ed)(1995) *Disability and Democracy: Reconstructing Special Education for Postmodernity*, Special Education Series (New York: Teachers College Press).

Snyder, S.L. and Mitchell, D. T. (2006) *Cultural Locations of Disability* (Chicago and London: The University of Chicago Press).

--------et al (Eds) (2002) *Disability Studies: Enabling the Humanities* (New York: Modern Language Association Press).

Sodak, L.C. (2003) *Classroom Management in Inclusive Settings* (Wiley- Blackwell).

Steinfeld, E. (1977) Major Issues in Developing Building Standards, In: Michael Bednars (Ed) *Barrier-Free Environments* (Stroudsburg, PA: Dowden, Hutchinson and Ross).

Stiker, H. (1999) *A History of Disability*, translated by W. Sayers (Ann Arbor: University of Michigan Press).

Stone, J.H. (Ed) (2005) *Culture and Disability: Providing Culturally Competent Services* (Thousand Oaks, CA: Sage).

Stone, E. and Priestly, M. (1996) Parasites, pawns and partners: Disability research and the role of non-disabled researchers, *British Journal of Sociology*, 47, pp. 699-716.

Stroman, D.F. (2003) *The Disability Rights Movement: From Deinstitutionalization to Self-determination* (Lanham, MD: University Press of America, Inc).

Svenson, K. (1994) The use of light rail or light rapid transit systems by individuals with severe visual impairment, *Journal of Vision Impairment and Blindness*, Jan-Feb.

Swain, J. et al (Eds)(2003) *Controversial Issues in a Disabling Society* (Sheffield: Open University Press).

--------(Eds) (1993) *Disabling Barriers Enabling Environments* (New Delhi: Sage Publications).

Swann, J.I. (2007) *Promoting independence and activity in older people* (Quay Books).

The Access Technology Handbook Giving visually impaired users access to your Disability Unit or ICT Laboratory (Sensory Solutions (Pty) Ltd, 2008); available at: http://www.sensorysolutions.co.za/PDF/GeneralInfo/The%20Disability%20Handbook%20-%20Volume%201%20-%20The%20ICT%20laboratory.pdf

The Second Regional Workshop on the Enhancement of Information and Communication Technology (ICT) Accessibility for Persons with Disabilities, held on 13-15 October 2009, Annex II; available at: www.unescap.org/ESID/Meetings/ICT09/Cam_R.pdf

Thiher, A. (2000) *Revels in Madness: Insanity in Medicine and Literature* (Ann Arbor: University of Michigan Press).

Thomas Barrie (2010) *The Sacred In-Between: The Mediating Roles of Architecture* (Routledge).

Thomas, C. (2002) The 'Disabled Body, In: Mary Evans and Ellie Lee (Eds) *Real Bodies: A Sociological Introduction* (New York: Palgrave).

Thomson, R.G. (1997) *Extraordinary Bodies: Figuring Physical Disability in American Culture and Literature* (New York: Columbia University Press).

--------(1996) *Freakery: Cultural Spectacles of the Extraordinary Body* (New York: New York University Press).

Tibbo H. (1991) Information systems, services and technology for the humanities, *Annual Review of Information Science and Technology* 26, pp. 287-346.

Titchkosky, Tanya (2007) *Reading & Writing Disability Differently: The Textured Life of Embodiment* (Toronto: University of Toronto Press).

--------(2006) *Disability, Self, and Society* (University of Toronto Press), rep.

Tobin, T. J. (2002) Issues in Preparing Visually Disabled Instructors to Teach Online: A Case Study, *Information Technology and Disabilities,* (8)(1), Special Issue: Distance Education and Disability, January.

Tornatsky, L. G., and Klein, K. J. (1982) Innovation characteristics and innovation adoption-implementation: A meta-analysis of findings, *IEEE Transactions on Engineering Management*, 29(1), pp. 28-45.

Tremain, S. (Ed) (1999) *Bodies of Knowledge: Critical Perspectives on Disablement and Disabled Women* (Toronto: Women's Press).

Tumlin, J. and Wolff-Heller, K. (2004) Using word prediction software to increase typing fluency with students with physical disabilities, *Journal of Special Education Technology, 19*(3).

Turner, D.M. and Stagg, Kevin (Eds) (2006a) *Social Histories of Disability and Deformity* (Oxon: Routledge).

United Nations (2007) From *Exclusion to Equality: Realizing the Rights of Persons with Disabilities*, Handbook for Parliamentarians on the Convention on the Rights of Persons with Disabilities and its Optional Protocol (Geneva).

--------(2006) *United Nations Convention on Rights of Persons with Disabilities* (New York: United Nations).

UNESCO (2009) eAccessibility ICT and Marginalised Youth (Geneva: Communication & Information Sector; available at: http://www.epractice.eu/en/library/300042.

UNESCO (undated) ICT and Disabled People; available at: http://portal.unesco.org/ci/en/ev.php-URL_ID=20486& URL_ DO=DO_P RINTPAGE&URL_ SECTION=201.html

Uys, L.R. and Gwele, N. (2005) *Curriculum Development in Nursing: Process and Innovations* (London and New York: Routledge.

Van der Heijden, D. (2007) How Does Alternative Access to Computers Work?, June 26.

Van Manen, Max (1990) *Researching Lived Experience: Human Science for an Action Sensitive Pedagogy* (London Ontario: Althouse Press).

Vash, Carolyn L. and Crewe, Nancy M. (2003) *Psychology of Disability* (New York: Springer Publishing Company), second edition

Veeger, H.E. J. et al (1989) Wheelchair propulsion technique at different speeds, *Scand J Rehab Med*; 21, pp. 197-203.

Verbrugge, L. and Sevak, P. (2002) Use, Type, and Efficacy of Assistance for Disability, *Journal of Gerontology Social Sciences*, 57B(6), pp. S366-S379.

Verma, G. K. et al (Eds) (2007) *International Perspectives on Educational Diversity and Inclusion: Studies from America,* Europe *and India* (Oxon: Routledge).

Verma, S. K. (Ed) (2002) *Rights of Persons with Disabilities* (New Delhi: Indian Law Institute).

Ville, I. et al (1994) Self-representations and physical impairment: a social constructionist approach, *Sociology of Health & Illness,* 16, pp. 301–321.

Wappett, Matthew and Arndt, Katrina (Eds)(2013) *Foundations of Disability Studies* (New York: Palgrave Macmillan).

Ware, L. (2004) *Ideology and the Politics of (In)Exclusion (*New York: Peter Lang).

Warrick, A. and S. Kaul (1997) *Their Manner of Speaking: Augmentative Communication for children and young adults with severe speech disorders* (Kolkata, India: Indian Institute of Cerebral Palsy).

--------(2002) *Everyone in Talking: Using Communication Displays* (Kolkata, India: Indian Institute of Cerebral Palsy).

Wassreman, D. et al (Eds) (2005) *Quality of Life and Human Difference* (Cambridge University Press).

Watermeyer, Brian (2013) *Towards a Contextual Psychology of Disablism* (London and New York: Routledge)

Watermeyer, B. et al (Eds) (2006) *Disability and Social Change: A South African Agenda* (Cape Town: HSRC Press).

Watson, Nick et al (2012) *Routledge Handbook of Disability Studies* (London and New York: Routledge)

Webster, J.G. et al (Eds) (1985) *Electronic Devices for Rehabilitation* (New York: John Wiley).

Weedman, J. (1993) On the "isolation" of humanists, *Communication Research*, 20(6), pp. 749-776.

Welsh, R.L. and Blasch, B.B. (1980) *Foundations of orientation and mobility* (New York: American Foundation for the Blind).

Wendell, S. (1996) *The Rejected Body: Feminist Philosophical Reflections on Disability* (New York: Routledge).

WHO (2001) *International Classification of Functioning, Disability, and Health (Geneva)*

--------(1980) *International Classification of Impairments, Disabilities, and Handicaps: A Manual of Classification Relating to the Consequences of Disease* (Geneva).

WHO and World Bank (2011) *World Report on Disability* (Geneva), also available at: http://www.who.int/disabilities/world_report/2011/report.pdf

Wiberley, S.E. (1991) Habits of humanists: Scholarly behavior and new information technologies, *Library Hi Tech*, 9(1), pp. 17-21.

Wijk, M. (1990) *European Manual for an Accessible Built Environment* (Utrecht: IG- Nederland).

Willmuth, M. and Holcomb, L. (1994) *Women with Disabilities: Found V*oices (Binghamton, NY: The Haworth Press, Inc).

Williams, P. et al (2007) ICTs and learning disability: multidisciplinary perspectives, Aslib Proceedings, 59 (1), pp. 97-112; available at: http://195.92.228.61/Insight/view ContentItem. do;jsessionid= A28E4B0D425210 C977700F3E6397E53B? content Type= Article&hd Action = lnkhtml&contentId=158 9313&history=false

Wilson, J.C. and Lewiecki-Wilson, C. (2001) *Embodied Rhetorics: Disability in Language and Culture* (Carbondale, IL:Southern Illinois Univ. Press).

Withers, A.J. (2012) *Disability Politics & Theory,* (Nova Scotia and Manitoba: Fernwood Publishing).

Wood, W.M. et al (1998) Using Distance Learning to Prepare Supported Employment Professionals, *Journal of Rehabilitation*, 64(3), pp. 48-53.

World Bank (2007a) *People with Disabilities in India: From Commitments to Outcomes* (New Delhi).

Wright, David (2011) *Downs: The History of a Disability* (OUP)

Wright, D. and Digby, A. (Eds) (2002) *From Idiocy to Mental Deficiency: Historical Perspectives on People with Learning Disabilities* (London: Routledge), rep.

Wrightson, W. (1989) *From Barrier Free to Safe Environments: the New Zealand Experience* (New York: World Rehabilitation Fund).

Zagler, W.L. and Panek, P. (1999) Assisting the Facilitators – Interface Design and Telematic Support for ITBased Assistive Technology, *Technology and Disability*, No. 10, pp. 129-136.

Zola, I. K. (2003) *Missing Pieces: A Chronicle of Living with a Disability* (Philadelphia: Temple University Press).

Selected Journals

- *ALTER. European Journal of Disability Research*
- *American Annals of the Deaf* (CEASDCAID: USA)
- *American Archives of Rehabilitation Therapy* (North Little Rock:USA)
- *American Corrective Therapy Journal* (San Diego, Calif: USA)
- *American Journal of Art Therapy* (Washington D. D. USA)
- *American Journal of Occupational Theraphy* (Roockville, Md.; USA)
- *American Journal of Physical Medicine* (Baltimore: USA)
- *American Journal on Intellectual and Developmental Disabilities*
- *American Rehabilitation* (Washington D.C.: USA)
- Amicus (Notre Dame: USA)
- *Archives of Physical Medicine and Rehabilitation* (Chicago: USA)
- *Australian Disability Review*
- *British Journal of Learning Disabilities*
- *Bulletin of Prosthetic Research* (Washington DC: USA)
- *Canadian Journal of Disability Studies*
- *Critical Disability Discourse*
- *Disability & Society*
- *Disability and Health Journal*
- *Disability and Rehabilitation*
- Disability and Rehabilitation
- *Disability and Rehabilitation: Assistive Technology*
- *Disability Studies Quarterly*
- *Focus on Autism and Other Developmental Disabilities*
- *Hearing Rehabilitation Quarterly* (North Holland)
- *International Journal of Disability Management*
- *International Journal of Disability Studies*
- *International Journal of Disability, Development and Education*
- *International Journal of Mental Health and Deafness*

- *International Journal of Rehabilitation Research* (Heidelberg; Germany)
- *International Journal on Disability and Human Development*
- *International Rehabilitation Medicine* (Basel: Switzerland)
- *International Rehabilitation Review* (New York: USA)
- *Journal of Applied Rehabilitation Counseling* (Fallschurch: USA)
- *Journal of Applied Research in Intellectual Disabilities*
- *Journal of Developmental and Physical Disabilities*
- *Journal of Disability Policy Studies*
- *Journal of Disability Policy Studies*
- *Journal of Disability Studies*
- *Journal of Intellectual & Developmental Disability*
- *Journal of Intellectual & Developmental Disability*
- *Journal of Intellectual Disabilities*
- *Journal of Intellectual Disabilities*
- *Journal of Intellectual Disability Research*
- *Journal of Learning Disabilities*
- *Journal of Learning Disabilities*
- *Journal of Learning Disabilities* (Glassboro, N.J.: USA)
- *Journal of Literary & Cultural Disability Studies*
- *Journal of Literary and Cultural Disability Studies*
- *Journal of Rehabilitation* (Alexandria, Va: USA)
- *Journal of Speech and Hearing Research* (Reckville Md.: USA)
- *Journal of Visual Impairment and Blindness* (New York: USA)
- *Learning Disabilities: A Contemporary Journal*
- *Learning Disability Practice*
- *Learning Disability Quarterly*
- *Physical Therapy* (Washington, DC: USA)
- *Physiotherapy* (London :UK)
- *Physiotherapy* (London: UK)
- *Physiotherapy Canada* (Toronto: Canada)

- *Prosthetics and Orthotics International* (Copenhagen: Holland)
- *Rehabilitation Digest* (Toronto, Ontario: Canada)
- *Rehabilitation in Australia* (Deakin)
- *Rehabilitation Literature*
- *Rehabilitation Psychology* (Washington DC: USA)
- Rehabilitation *World* (New York: USA)
- *Research in Developmental Disabilities*
- *Scandinavian Journal of Rehabilitation Medicine* (Stockholm: Sweden)
- *Sexuality and Disability* (New York: USA).
- *Technology and Disability*
- The *Canadian Journal of Occupation Therapy* (Toronto: Canada)
- *The deaf American* (NAD: USA)
- *The Review of Disability Studies an International Journal*

Index

❑❑❑❑❑